BLINDSPOTS

BLINDSPOTS

THE MANY WAYS WE CANNOT SEE

BRUNO G. BREITMEYER

OXFORD
UNIVERSITY PRESS

2010

OXFORD
UNIVERSITY PRESS

Oxford University Press, Inc., publishes works that further
Oxford University's objective of excellence
in research, scholarship, and education.

Oxford   New York
Auckland   Cape Town   Dar es Salaam   Hong Kong   Karachi
Kuala Lumpur   Madrid   Melbourne   Mexico City   Nairobi
New Delhi   Shanghai   Taipei   Toronto

With offices in
Argentina   Austria   Brazil   Chile   Czech Republic   France   Greece
Guatemala   Hungary   Italy   Japan   Poland   Portugal   Singapore
South Korea   Switzerland   Thailand   Turkey   Ukraine   Vietnam

Copyright © 2010 by Oxford University Press

Published by Oxford University Press, Inc.
198 Madison Avenue, New York, New York 10016

www.oup.com

Oxford is a registered trademark of Oxford University Press

Library of Congress Cataloging-in-Publication Data
Breitmeyer, Bruno G.
Blindspots : the many ways we cannot see / Bruno G. Breitmeyer.
   p.   cm.
Includes bibliographical references and index.
ISBN 978-0-19-539426-9
1. Visual perception.   I. Title.
BF241.B728 2010
152.14—dc22
2009029990

1   3   5   7   9   8   6   4   2

Printed in China

There are four kinds of men who are good, and the four love me Arjuna: the man of sorrows, the seeker of knowledge, the seeker of something he treasures, and the man of vision. The greatest of these is the man of vision, who is ever one, who loves the One. For I love the man of vision, and the man of vision loves me.

Bhagavad Ghita (Krishna speaking)

PREFACE

During my first year of graduate studies in the psychology department of Stanford University, I enrolled in a seminar on visual perception. Although I barely passed the seminar, I found it to be immensely engaging and interesting. Since then I have "viewed" the study of visual perception as an experimental epistemology, the study of how we come to know the world around us. We see within a "lumisphere," much like we breathe within an atmosphere: with little or no effort, thought, or reflection. Just as the myriad physiological processes that support normal breathing (and that breathing supports) proceed without our intention or willful planning, so normal vision by and large also proceeds with ease—unless special circumstances interfere with it. The philosopher José Ortega Y Gasset noted how such special circumstances, often unexpected and sometimes troubling, can stir us from metaphysical slumber as vigorously as Immanuel Kant was stirred after reading the philosophical treatises of David Hume. They can force us to review some of our basic presuppositions about the world that we inhabit.

I recall a particular conversation I had about two decades ago with a young female bartender at one of my favorite and, alas, long dried-up watering holes in Houston. She happened to be a former computer science student who had graduated from Rice University. After she popped the cap from a bottle of Shiner beer, our conversation zeroed in on our respective careers. I told her that I was an experimental psychologist in the Department of Psychology at the University of Houston and that my specialty was the study of vision, of how we see. Her response was quick and a bit condescending, "Why study it? All you have to do is open your eyes." Initially baffled, I realized how true such a response sounded from the perspective of a visually "normal" lay person, yet how false from several other perspectives.

My response to her took two tacks. First, I suggested that if she were correct, how would she explain the behavior of millions of people who, despite having eyes open, must visit an optometrist, ophthalmologist or neurologist for treatment of their problems with seeing. Second, I followed up on her computer science background and asked her whether seeing well or playing chess well was the harder task for her. She replied that, of course, playing chess was more difficult, since it depends on strategic multimove planning, knowledge of tactical maneuvers, countermoves, and so forth, all of which required a constant level of alertness, concentration, and effort directed not only to the changing configurations of the chessboard but also to the many reserves of chess expertise accumulated and stored in memory. I then asked her to imagine herself as a crack computer hack faced with the task of developing two types of artificial intelligence machines: one that could play chess as well as a chess master, the other that could see as well as a healthy adult human being. Given these two alternatives, she agreed with me that programming a seeing machine would be much more difficult than programming a chess-playing machine.

Vision, the ability to process information transmitted by the medium of light, and for that matter other sensory modalities like audition, appear to be deceptively simple—unless . . . . And when the ellipsis is filled in with any one of uncountable caveats, its suspended complexities crystallize. In the following chapters I will fill in the ellipsis by introducing the reader, in Part I, to various kinds of blindness, of failures to see, whose causes range from natural design constraints to poor optics, flaws in neural processing, and various types of transient blindness induced in the vision laboratory. In Part II, I will cover "blindness borderlands" by discussing two classes of neurological deficits that dwell along the borders between visuosensory and visuoconceptual domains, the latter type of blindness impinging on the "mind's eye." This will segue into coverage, in Part III, of various kinds of cognitive ways of not seeing, some attributable to the technical and essential expressions of art, others to cognitive blind spots or reasoning bloopers to which all of us can fall prey, and still others to the blunders and blinkers of cultural and personal biases. For those readers who want to learn more about the topics covered in this book, I have included a list of suggested readings at the end of this book.

I have intended to write such an exposé of blindnesses for more than two decades now but have been delayed by other time-consuming projects. This proved to be my fortune, for the delay allowed me to integrate increasing amounts of scholarly and experimental vision research into my reflections on the theme of blindness. That said, this is not a book about how scientific research in an area like vision works, nor is it intended for the specialist in vision. It is much too cursory in its treatment of substantive topics and more anecdotal than is typical of an academic book. Moreover, it addresses vision and blindness in their broadest sense: Beyond their literal meanings, words like "sight" and "illumination" or "blindness" and "darkness" and their cognates are universal metaphors for realms of discovery and comprehension on the one hand and of ignorance and misunderstanding on the other. They are, in short, words that both the vision scientist and the individual engaged in creative work use. For that reason, the book is meant to appeal to the educated and interested lay person who may be curious not only about how vision works and how various blindnesses affect it, but also about how "seeing" and "blindness" apply to a wider range of cognitions. After all, in various senses we see with our eyes, our minds, and our hearts. So as the book progresses, I initially don my scientific hat but then gradually remove it as I finally nod to the humanities in my exploration of the various ways we do and do not see. I have much enjoyed writing this book, and I hope that reading it provides equal pleasure to you.

In this compendium of topics with a theme, I have drawn both on some of my own work, particularly in later parts of the book, and on the difficult and creative work accomplished in diverse areas of study by numerous scientists and scholars, some of whom I know personally, but most of whom I can acknowledge as colleagues only through their work. Without naming them, I collectively and collegially thank all for their contributions to this book. Here I should say that I am far from being an expert in all the cognitive sciences. For that reason and because this book is somewhat of a fly-over covering much terrain, my treatment of its particular features occasionally may be in error. If so, I hope the errors are not too egregious. If I have misinterpreted or misrepresented a particular individual's statements, I proactively take blame and ask for pardon.

I would also like to acknowledge my debt to Catharine Carlin and Nicholas Liu of Oxford University Press for their encouragement and editorial assistance. Special thanks go to Marion Osmun. Her careful reading and rewriting of the original manuscript has reduced jargon to a minimum, eliminated redundancies, typographical and syntactical errors, and clarified phrasings, all rendering the book much more accessible to the nonexpert than it otherwise would have been. Thanks also to the Small Grants Program and the psychology department of the University of Houston for financially supporting the acquisition of images and reproduction rights of many of the illustrations included in this book.

Finally, I would like to dedicate this book in loving memory of my brother Alex and my nephew Daniel. May the scales of blindness be lifted from their eyes forever.

BGB
Houston, Texas
March 2009

CONTENTS

XIII

PART I

BLINDNESS CORPOREAL

nihil est in intellectu, quod non sit prius in sensu
(Nothing is in the understanding that first is not in sensation.)

ARISTOTLE, *DE ANIMA*

Vision is one of several senses that allow us to pick up information from and about our environment. Our capacity for visual cognition is vast, yet limited by several factors. These factors include the functional design of the visual apparatus, from the eye to the brain, and any inherited or acquired defects of that design. Although some of these constraints can be loosened by special aids or circumvented by compensatory processes, they indicate how intricate and complex the superficially simple act of visual cognition is. And oddly enough, the limits placed on our visual cognition can occasion an expansion of our body of knowledge.

ONE

A Brief History of Vision and Blindness

Yond Cassius has a lean and hungry look
WILLIAM SHAKESPEARE, *JULIUS CAESAR*

When average readers think about how vision works, they think of it simply as a transparent process that allows us to receive information about the world transmitted through the medium of light. Such a passive view of vision is common, but it is only partly correct. Vision is a very active process—one that is as much in pursuit of something as it is in receipt of something. In fact, according to one hypothetical scenario, it evolved from "predatory" behavior of single-celled organisms, akin to cyanobacteria, that "hunted" light for its nutritive (energy) value, much like animals forage for plants or hunt other animals for sustenance. According to this evolutionary tale, protocells initially survived on the murky but energy-rich soup composed of amino acids and other organic molecules clouding the surface waters on our primeval earth. As the bounteous food supply in the earth's surface waters was progressively depleted by an exploding population of these protocells, the need for additional sources of nutrient energy increased. Fortunately for our eventual evolution, as the biotic soup thinned, progressively more sunlight was able to penetrate earth's waters, allowing some of these organisms near the water's surface to develop photoreactive molecules as a means of capturing and "digesting" the readily available and energy-rich quanta (photons) of light. These proto-cells were precursors not only of photosynthetic organisms, ancestors of our plants, but much later also of the photosensitive receptors found in the newly evolving eyes that drove the explosive speciation of animals during the Cambrian period some 600 million years ago.

The eyes of these Cambrian species evolved in two interesting ways. First, they were located at the organism's "front end," conveniently near the feeding apparatus that stuffed foods into these creatures' maws. Second, the eyes contained very many (from hundreds to millions) photoreceptors. Thus, at vision's front end, a densely packed array of photoreceptors (e.g., like the rods and cones in the human eye) could simultaneously (in parallel) "monitor" a large part of the lumisphere (the part of the biosphere that relies in one way or another on light) for informative objects and events—a feat that an organism with a single photoreceptor was (and still is) capable of accomplishing only through a very time-consuming, bit-by-bit (sequential) "scanning" of the environment. Elevated from being merely a nutrient source that supported the energy needs for "grunt" work, light would henceforth be enrolled as a very efficient medium for "feeding" an animal's more classy "brain" power with a huge flux of information that adaptively supported more sophisticated and more violent forms of consummatory behaviors: nutritional predation, the at times lethal but usually softened violence of sexual pursuit, and, of course, the usually more benign pursuit of shelter from predators and hostile forces of nature.

All animals with complex nervous systems, including fish, are believed to have evolved from the Cambrian creatures. Some of these early fish, akin to the extant Caelacanth, evolved protolimbs in place of their fins, allowing them not only to steer through the water but, along the subsequent steps of evolution, also to waddle along the bottom of their aquatic world. Some of these, specifically the lung fish, in turn evolved protolungs, allowing them to forsake the lowly status of bottom feeders and to waddle additionally onto land for extended durations to feast on the increasing variety of meals *du jour*. And so it went until *voilà*, on a geological time scale, protohumans evolved during the blink of an eye (no pun intended) into the modern humans we are today—some of us oversexed, -fed, -attired, and -housed as we set our sights on continuing the (in some nations, constitutionally guaranteed) pursuit of sex, food, and shelter, together with the tokens some of us associate with these ends: sexy and powerful cars, oil to fuel them, two-car garages, and homeland security to shelter our way of life.

This eat-or-be-eaten romp through the history of sight is offered tongue in cheek. But at a more serious level, besides helping us to sustain the material base that supports life, vision gratuitously confers several other benefits. It augments and enlivens our mental, emotional, and spiritual lives. It affords the superabundant delights of reading, study, and exploration; of appreciating the beauties of nature, architecture, and the arts; of partaking in the thrills of theatric, operatic, or cinematic drama; of finding refuge in the serene splendor of plangent shores, shimmering deserts, or majestic mountains. It serves us for any of these purposes, with their offshoots sometimes flourishing into excess. Consequently, the loss or limit of even a part of our vision usually poses problems and causes grief.

The degrees of absence or loss of vision that we call partial or complete blindness constitute the ways we don't see. These ways have their own natural and cultural history. Were we to write such a "negative" natural history, we would note that many organisms might never have evolved photosensitivity of any kind, let alone one we can call visual. Organisms living in the depths of the ocean rely mostly on sensitivity to chemical or mechanical stimulation. Likewise, several varieties of albino fish found in ocean depths or in dark freshwater caverns and some land mammals like the mole presumably evolved from organisms that at one time had well-developed vision. Gradually they lost it, since it no longer served adaptive survival strategies in the aquatic depths or in the sub-terranean world. Instead, the chemical senses akin to smell and taste; the mechanical sense of touch, activated, for example, by the vibrissae (long stiff hairs) near the nose and mouth of a mole; the heightened mechanical sense of audition in nocturnal mammals, such as the bat; and the electrical sense in some fish, such as the electric eel—any of these, alone or in combination, can guide an animal to food or a mate and alert it to danger.

We can also inferentially draw evidence for the historic existence of other forms of natural blindness, particularly those afflicting humans, by extrapolating from current cases of vision loss. It is highly unlikely that cataracts, myopia, hyperopia, detached retinas, congenital blindness, and other such visual defects are entirely recent afflictions—that is, those occurring only since about 500 years ago, when, for instance, an explosion of printed materials made reliance on close-up, myopic reading a necessity—rather than ones that also occurred in the more distant historic and prehistoric past. Moreover, since life has always been a high-risk enterprise, there must also have been plenty of individuals who lost partial or total vision to diseases like glaucoma and macular degeneration or to the accidental severing of the optic nerve and destruction of visual areas of the brain by a projectile penetrating the skull. Indeed, medical treatises going back at least two millennia record a variety of naturally and accidentally induced blindness. There are also historic accounts of eye enucleations performed as punishment for certain crimes. Christian Scripture contains accounts of miraculous healings of blindness, as do other sacred traditions.

As to a cultural (or social) history of blindness, I suspect that much of it can be summarized by a muted version of the biblical admonition to remove the beam in one's own eye before judging another for the mote in his or hers. As will become evident in later chapters, culture can affect how we see and fail to see by influencing both our choices of what we attend to or ignore visually and our interpretations of visual stimuli that we do choose to attend to. For instance, in some past cultures, it was considered a blatant breach of decorum if not a crime for a commoner to look at, let alone make eye contact with, a person of powerful social, political, or religious rank. During the encounter with the high-rank individual, the commoner would effectively be blind to the nuances of facial expression that are such an important part of social communication. As another example, fluctuating cultural fashions have shaped the changing criteria for visually assessing the corporeal beauty of women. Based on the criteria in vogue during a particular era, the (male) gaze may ignore straight or curly hair, small or large breasts, flat or rounded tummy, and so on. Moreover, even when we direct our gaze at the same object, visual cognizing differs radically among members of different cultures. The cross, seen two millennia ago throughout the Roman Empire as a symbol of an ignominious end (i.e., crucifixion), was some 300 years later seen as a symbol of triumphant hope, and some centuries later by other empires as a symbol of brutal infidels.

Finally, cross-cultural comparative studies have revealed the effects of cultural bias on perceptual differences not only at these higher, interpretive levels of visual cognition, but also at relatively lower, sensory stages of processing in the visual system. Culturally biased perceptual differences occur, for example, even in simple line orientation and line length discriminations, tasks once thought to rely on hardwired physiological processes that are largely immune to cultural influences. Since such differences no doubt existed in eras prior to our own, they potentially also belong to the larger cultural history of seeing and not seeing.

I will discuss in greater depth these and other factors underlying blindness in later chapters. For now, let's turn to the rest of Part I of the book and examine in more detail some of the natural—that is, the physical, biological, and ecological—constraints that can blinker our vision.

TWO

Our Inheritance

Functional Constraints on "Normal" Vision

W e humans are one of millions of species of animals with visual systems, each of which have their own capabilities and unique design constraints. They can be found anywhere from the front end, for example, the optical structure of the eye, to the back end, for example, the neural architecture of the brain. The design of each organism's visual system is adapted to its particular ecological niche, from, say, the relatively simple visual system of a frog concerned chiefly with basic biological survival and reproduction to our many additional visual engagements with complex processes of civilization and culture. To illustrate the limits or blind areas in our vision, I will compare our visual system to those of other animals.

PLAYING HIDE AND SEEK

There is one limit on vision that applies to all creatures with visual systems. What we call "light" is a type of electromagnetic radiation restricted to a specific range of wavelengths within the entire electro-magnetic spectrum that runs from extremely short-wavelength gamma rays to the very long radio waves. The chemical properties of light-sensitive pigments found in our retinal receptors limit the response of these receptors to wavelengths of about 4×10^{-7} to 7×10^{-7} meters. Although other seeing creatures might be responsive to a slighter wider or narrower range of wavelengths, their vision, like ours, is blind to wavelengths falling outside a specified range. Moreover, all vision is limited by the fact that the wavelengths within a specified range do not pass through certain types of materials. This physical property renders such materials opaque to light. In a natural environment, opaqueness to light typically is correlated both with reflection of light from the surfaces of these materials and with their impenetrability. Similarly, transparency to light is usually associated with penetrability. These coincidences allow us on the one hand to see, and avoid collision with, objects that we approach (a wall or other obstruction) or that approach us (an object thrown at us) and on the other hand to pass through unobstructed spaces.

These coincidences can have both fortunate and unfortunate consequences. If you stand behind an opaque obstruction, you escape the visual scrutiny of others, thus guarding your privacy or perhaps even hiding from others who may be intent on harming you. But you also cannot see events or objects behind the opaque obstruction that you might need to see (e.g., a person behind a door as you or he pushes it open) or want to see (e.g., the contents of a gift-wrapped package you are not allowed to open). Likewise, transparency and mechanical penetrability can pose their own misfortunes. Perhaps, for example, you have seen a bird crash into a window pane—sometimes a minor mishap in which the bird is temporarily stunned, and sometimes a severe accident in which the bird breaks its beak or wing or even dies. Once I helplessly watched as one of my colleagues walked into a glass door of a restaurant; he was stunned but otherwise suffered no bodily damage. I also have bumped into glass partitions on rare occasions, suffering nothing more than embarrassment. Since here the expected coincidence between surface transparency and mechanical penetrability is upset, these mishaps demonstrate that surface impenetrability at times cannot be seen without the co-occurrence of surface opaqueness (e.g., a visible glaze or a sign on the glass partition that alerts one to its impenetrability).

THE HARES HAVE IT—OR DO THEY?

Imagine the following scene. On a quiet sunny afternoon, a rabbit is munching on a crisp, juicy carrot among the many other forbidden delectables in Mr. Jones's well-groomed vegetable garden. The Edenic setting is disturbed when Mr. Jones slowly sneaks up behind the rabbit, ready to whack it with a short rake. However, before he is even remotely within striking distance, the rabbit scurries off to safety. Now consider this scene. You are at the edge of Mr. Jones's flower garden and are contemplating the array of colorful blossoms. Approaching you from behind, within arm's reach, he remarks, "Beautiful, aren't they?" You startle before giving a delayed "Sure are."

Why does the rabbit have literal hindsight that allows it to detect Mr. Jones at an appreciable distance behind it while you are blind to his presence at a shorter distance? Because the rabbit's eyes are located laterally, at the sides of its head, while yours are located at the front of your head. This difference, shown in Figure 2.1, confers on the rabbit a wide-angle, panoramic view of the world that includes most of what is located behind it but confers on you a narrower-angle, frontal view of the world, effectively rendering you blind to what is behind you. Eye placement similar to that of a rabbit is found in many other animals, from the tiny frogs in your garden

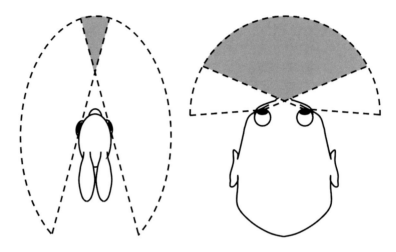

Figure 2.1. Schematic depictions of monocular (white) and binocular (gray) portions of the visual fields of a rabbit (left) and of a human (right).

pond to the massive water buffalo at a watering hole in the African steppes. Since their typical defense against threat is flight rather than fight, these animals must visually monitor as much of their surrounding world as possible for the potential entry of predators. In contrast, our narrower-angle, frontal vision renders us and other creatures like cats, monkeys, and the great apes, "retroblind".

However, relative visual disadvantages such as these are often accompanied by advantages and vice versa. Note also in Figure 2.1 that the head positions of a human's eyes afford a much larger frontal binocular field of view than do the positions of the rabbit's eyes. For that reason among others, human binocular vision, especially stereoscopic depth perception, is keener and more extensive than that of the rabbit, rendering the rabbit stereoblind relative to us (more on stereoblindness in humans later). So for both frontal-eye and lateral-eye creatures, there are relative gains and losses of visual competence.

AT TIMES MORE ACTUALLY IS BETTER

Let us now consider how another design feature limits visual performance. Every seeing creature can be regarded as having a design property called limited receptivity. As mentioned, visible light is a type of electromagnetic radiation whose wavelength ranges from about 4×10^{-7} to 7×10^{-7} meters. Just below the wavelengths of our visual spectrum are the short ultraviolet ones, and just above are the infrared ones. Consequently, we cannot see objects reflecting only ultraviolet and shorter wavelengths or those reflecting only infrared and longer wavelengths. In contrast, a honeybee's eyes or those of the kestrel, a raptor bird, are known to have receptors sensitive to ultraviolet rays. The bee's (limited) receptivity, extending as it does to short ultraviolet wavelengths, allows the bee to detect the central portion of flowers containing pollen and nectar. The kestrel uses its ultraviolet receptivity to locate the telltale urine stains of rodents. Other organisms are sensitive to infrared radiation. For example, rattlesnakes, a type of pit viper (so called because they have a small infrared- or heat-sensitive "pit" next to each of their eyes), can detect the location of a small mammal radiating its infrared body heat into the cool desert night. Unaided human vision is blind to ultraviolet or infrared light. Only with current technology—for instance, with films sensitive to short-wavelength ultraviolet and X-rays, with infrared-sensitive night vision goggles worn by soldiers on night patrol, and with radio telescopes used in astronomy—can we achieve the receptivity of these various animals and compensate our blindnesses to ultraviolet and shorter and to infrared and longer wavelengths.

Some animals, like the tarsier of Southeast Asia (see Fig. 2.2) or the fruit bat, are primarily nocturnal creatures. Besides other design features, their large eyes, containing only (or mainly) retinal rod receptors, are specialized for night vision. Although their vision is very good during a moonlit night, their daytime vision is very poor.

Figure 2.2. The large-pupiled eyes of the tarsier, a nocturnal animal.
Image © Animals Animals / Earth Scenes, Chatham, NY. Photo credit: Michael Dick.

Our eyes contain a very large number of cone receptors that allow us to see many things during the day that we cannot see at night. For that reason nocturnal creatures are day blind relative to diurnal (day-and-night) creatures like us. Their day vision is severely limited by their inability to distinguish among the many hues or wavelengths that we can discriminate, and their visual acuity, the ability to see fine spatial details like those required to thread a needle or to count the few hairs still growing on top of my head, is much poorer than ours.

Nachts sind alle Katzen grau ("At night all cats are gray") goes a German saying, indicating that humans effectively become rod monochromats at night: the rich palette of colors seen during the day transforms into a bland collection of a few dull gradations of gray at night. In addition, our nighttime visual acuity is very poor and all but nonexistent when we gaze directly at specific locations. This fact led astronomers prior to the invention of telescopes to sight small and faint heavenly bodies by looking at them askance rather than directly. What design features of our visual system contribute to this odd way of observing the constellations of faint celestial objects with our naked eyes?

First, the fovea, the central portion of the human retina on which objects at the center of our gaze project their images, contains no rod receptors. Thus at night, when illumination levels are generally too low to activate the millions of cones that are densely arrayed in the foveal and immediately adjacent, perifoveal regions of the retina, we basically are blind to the very low levels of light that impinge on these regions of the retina from very distant stars. Second, the concentration of rod receptors is highest (roughly $150,000/mm^2$ of retina) about 15° to 20° or so from the fovea. In view of these two features (see Fig. 2.3), it should be evident why astronomers, viewing very distant celestial objects with the unaided eye, did so by directing their gaze (about 10°–20°) askance, thus effectively recruiting that concentration of rod receptors.

Compared to the tarsier and other nocturnal animals that have few, if any, cones, we are endowed with millions of cones. So let's return to daytime, when the cone receptors in our eyes are at work and the rods are "shut down for the day." Although during the day our abilities to discriminate spatial details and hues are much better than those of a tarsier, they are not equally good throughout our visual fields. You may have noticed that when you direct your gaze at an object, its form and color appear distinct and sharp while those of objects at increasing distances beyond your directed gaze appear

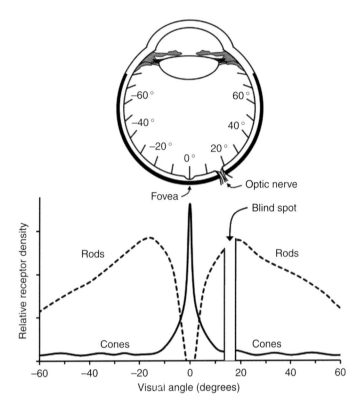

Figure 2.3. Top: Schematic of the human eye showing the fovea of the retina and the optic nerve. Bottom: The relative density of cone and rod receptors as a function of distance from the fovea (in degrees visual angle).

progressively less well defined and clear. Why? Several structural and functional features contribute this differential sensitivity to an object's form and color across the visual field:

1. In more complex eyes like ours, the tiny foveal region forms a "pit" in the retina. This pit displaces much of the retinal

neural tissue intervening between the incoming light and the foveal cone receptors, thus allowing the cone receptors in the fovea to have more direct access to the incoming light than do cone (or rod) receptors located outside the fovea.

2. In nonfoveal retinal areas, the shapes of the segments containing the light-sensitive pigments of cones (and rods) tend to be cylindrical. In contrast, in the center of the fovea, these cone segments are actually shaped like cones. This confers on each foveal cone what is known as a directional waveguide property, that is, the ability to effectively respond to light entering the cone-shaped segments along their main axes. Thereby each foveal cone is specialized to respond maximally to light entering the eye along a single direction and thus from a particular external locus. An analogy would be the cone-shaped hearing aid devices used many years ago by hearing-impaired individuals to guide sound waves arriving at the outer ear from the location of their external source.

3. The 10 million or so cone receptors in each eye are not evenly distributed over the retina. Their packing is densest in the center of the fovea (known as the foveola) and drops precipitously as the distance from the fovea increases. In fact, at a distance of about 10° from the fovea, the concentration attains its lowest value and remains at that value throughout the remainder of the retina.

4. Via intermediate neurons in the retina, the foveal cones connect to a single retinal ganglion cell (and sometimes to two of them). Each retinal ganglion cell in turn connects via tiny nerve fibers known as axons to the higher visual areas in the brain. You can think of a cone in the center of the fovea as having a "private line" (or sometimes even two of them) to the higher brain areas. In contrast, at increasing distances from the fovea, progressively more cone receptors connect to or converge on a single ganglion

cell. Hence, they have "shared lines" to the higher brain centers. Unlike the distinct visual "messages" arriving at higher brain centers from the foveal cones, the messages arriving at these brain centers from nonfoveal cones are not separable from each other. This results in less distinct vision outside the foveal region of the visual field.

5. The primary visual cortex, so called because it is the first cortical area to be activated by the signals projecting to it from the retinae of the two eyes, is characterized by a design feature called *cortical magnification*. This refers to the fact that the projections from the central, foveal region of each retina end up being processed by a disproportionately large part of the primary visual cortex as compared to projections from other, more peripheral areas of the retina.

6. The foveal part of the visual field usually corresponds not only to the anatomical center of vision but typically also to its attentional center. For example, throughout the typing of my manuscript up to now, my center of gaze and my center of attention both followed the cursor as it moved from left to right. But this coupling between the anatomical fovea and the "attentional fovea" is not invariable: under special circumstances, the center of spatial attention can be voluntarily dissociated from the center of gaze. While I typed this sentence on my computer screen, for example, I fixed my gaze at the left margin of each line yet directed my attention to the blinking cursor as the successively typed letters proceeded toward the right margin of the line.

All six of these structural, anatomical, and functional factors contribute to clearest and most acute vision in the center of the visual field. You can think of the entire visual field as consisting of an "island of sight" surrounded, relatively speaking, by a "sea of blindness." Imagine in particular a circular volcanic island. At the very center is the tip of the volcano corresponding to the area of sharpest vision. As you descend the slope of the volcano, vision becomes progressively coarser until you reach the vast ocean of coarsest vision.

However, lest you think that increasing distances from the center of gaze confer only a relative loss of vision, I should note that the ability to detect rapid motion or sudden changes of stimulation is actually very good and at times even better in the periphery of the visual field than in the central foveal region. Recall that the ability to detect movement or sudden changes is a very useful property of a rabbit's panoramic visual field. It is also a useful property in our less panoramic visual field. We also need to be alerted to changes in our peripheral visual field. Who knows— these changes might signal the presence of anything from friend to food to foe.

Although our spatial acuity is very good—better by about a factor of 10 than that of a cat—it is poor when compared to that of raptors. An object that we can barely see during the daytime at a distance of 300 feet, a peregrine falcon can detect at three times that distance, a feat that makes it a superb predator of small rodents, even from dizzying heights. For us to attain such spatial resolution, we again would have to rely on technology—that is, at long range on the aid of a telescope, and at short range, on a microscope. Additionally, the normal human is blind to wavelength differences that are visible to birds such as the pigeon or fish such as the trout. To attain their wavelength discrimination abilities, we need retinal receptors that are sensitive to ultraviolet light. More about this in the following chapter, where we take a brief look, among other things, at color vision and its defects.

ALL OF US HAVE A BLIND SPOT OR TWO

If you inspect Figure 2.3 carefully, you will note that about 15°–20° from the fovea is a small region of the retina where the optic nerve (made up of axons of the million or so retinal ganglion cells) exits the eye to progress toward higher visual areas of the brain. Because it contains no photoreceptors responding to light, this part of the retina is called the *blind spot*. Despite its presence, we normally do not notice a corresponding blind region in the images we see in our visual field. One reason is that the blind spot in one eye corresponds to a retinal region in the other eye that does contain rods and cones. Hence, the visual areas of the brain receive retinal input from at least one of the eyes. But even a person who has lost vision entirely in one eye does not normally notice a blind spot in her visual field. The reason for this is a process known as perceptual "filling-in," which we do not understand completely but which is believed to rely on sophisticated properties of neural activity in higher brain areas.

We can demonstrate the existence of the blind spot and of perceptual filling in according to the principle illustrated in Figure 2.4a. First, we want to establish a viewing condition so that the small black dot on the left of Figure 2.4b projects onto the blind spot of only one of the eyes, in this case the left eye. (If you prefer to use your right eye for these demonstrations, simply turn the book upside down and follow analogous instructions for the inverted displays.) Hold the book upright. While closing your right eye, fixate the cross (+) shown on the right of Figure 2.4b with your left eye. While keeping your gaze on the +, slowly and steadily move the book toward or away from you. Eventually you will find a viewing distance at which the black dot will disappear from view (you might simultaneously also have to rotate the book slightly to the left or right to establish the optimal viewing condition). If so, you have succeeded in locating the blind spot in your left eye.

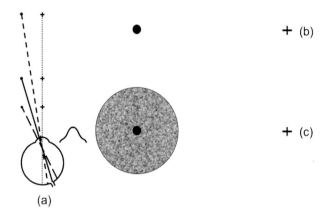

Figure 2.4. (a) The principle behind detecting the blind spot. With the right eye closed, the left eye must be at just the right distance from the display for the image of the black dot (to the left of a fixation cross) to fall on the blind spot of the left eye. (b) By varying the distance of the page while you fixate on the cross with your left eye (right eye closed), you should find a distance where the black dot to the left of fixation disappears from view. (c) Here the black dot should again disappear. Note, however, that you do not perceive a "hole" in your visual field; rather, the area in your visual field corresponding to the blind spot is "filled in" by the textured background.

Now, to demonstrate perceptual filling in, fixate the center of the + shown on the right of Figure 2.4c, and again move the book back and forth until the black dot on the textured background in Figure 2.4c disappears (since the black dot now again projects onto the blind spot of the left eye). Notice, however, that you don't actually see a hole in your visual field where the blind spot is located; the area in your perceptual field corresponding to it is filled in with the surrounding texture. It is as though the higher visual centers in the brain "assume" that the visual stimulation impinging on the blind spot of the retina has the same properties as that falling on its surrounding region, thereby filling in the blind spot with the perceptual properties found in the surrounding region.

EXCUSE ME! I DIDN'T SEE YOU SITTING THERE

One sunny Saturday in Houston, I decided to catch a matinee showing of a movie. Arriving late, I rushed into the movie theater, which was dark except for the dim light given by the previews on the screen and by the Art Deco fixtures on the side walls. The theater appeared not too crowded. I nudged along one of the rear rows of seats, and just as I was about to lower myself into a seat, a voice from the dark complained, "Hey dude, can'tcha see I'm sitt'n here?" Oops. Having been trained in the basics of visual perception, I should have known better than to hurriedly find a seat in the darkened theater. Why so?

Our visual system's sensitivity is at the mercy of variable environmental conditions. During the diurnal cycle, the overall level of ambient illumination changes slowly from the very low levels at night, through the moderate levels at dawn, the very high levels at noon, and the moderate levels at dusk, before returning to the very low levels at night. In order to maintain optimal sensitivity to luminance contrast (the difference between dark and light regions, e.g., between the dark print and white background of this text), the visual system must be capable of adjusting to these various changes in illumination. These adjustments are known as light adaptation when the overall level of illumination increases (e.g., from predawn to noon) and dark adaptation when the overall level decreases (e.g., from noon to postdusk). These adjustments, made at the photopigment level of individual receptors and at later postreceptor neural levels, typically occur slowly and for that reason go unnoticed during the normal course of a daily cycle.

However, when the change of overall illumination is sudden or very rapid, our visual system's adaptive mechanisms respond too sluggishly to keep up with the change, thus rendering us temporarily "blind" until the adjustment process has been completed. Dark adaptation is at a particular disadvantage since it proceeds more slowly than light adaptation. For instance, after leaving the dark theater to reenter the sunny outdoors, I very briefly suffered from a glarelike blinding effect before returning to an optimal level of visual sensitivity. In contrast, when I entered the dark theater from a sunny outdoors, my visual system remained insensitive or effectively blind to luminance contrasts for an appreciably longer time. Hence, my near *faux pas*. After I found an empty seat, I noticed a minute or so later that the theater was not as empty of viewers as it initially appeared to me. By now my vision had fully adapted to the overall dark surrounding, and I was able to see much more of the theater's interior than previously.

The upshot of the topics discussed in this chapter is that the visual abilities of a normal, healthy human, although at times better than those of some creatures, are worse than those of others. Thus, because of the way our visual system evolved, we are blind to features in the environment that are visible to these other creatures. However, because we rarely, if ever, compare our visual abilities to those of other organisms, we disregard these types of blindness. They are the norm, and therefore we do not regard them as problems. Problems arise, however, with the discovery that some of us cannot see things in our environment that other humans can see. Such types of blindness, caused by a variety of factors, are the subject of the next two chapters.

THREE

OUR MISINHERITANCE
Blindness I

I live among vague, luminous shapes that are not darkness yet.
In my eyes there are no days.

JORGE LUIS BORGES, *IN PRAISE OF DARKNESS*

An organism's development before birth is subject to the roll of genetic and epigenetic dice. For that reason, the visual capacities of a baby can be limited at birth by hereditary and congenital factors. These interact with environmental factors to plot the course of subsequent, postbirth development. The vision impairments resulting from flaws of prebirth development can be so mild as not to even be noticed or so profound as to render an individual totally blind. Very rare examples of the latter, absolute blindness are found in babies lacking eyes. In this chapter, I will briefly list and characterize other congenital and hereditary blindnesses and cover a few additional visual dysfunctions in greater detail. They comprise a class of total or partial blindnesses afflicting individuals whom many of us may have encountered in mundane, nonclinical settings.

PRELIMINARIES OF PHYSIOLOGICAL OPTICS

Optically a camera and an eye share structural and functional similarities. Both have adjustable optical elements that can refract light so as to yield on their respective light-sensitive pigment layers a sharply focused image of objects. The "lens" of a high-grade camera is actually made of an ensemble of optical elements, each of fixed refractive power, whose distance from the image plane of the film can be adjusted so as to sharply focus images of objects lying at variable distances from the camera. As shown in Figure 3.1, in the human eye, the cornea can be thought of as a fixed-power lens that performs most of the refraction of light, which is subsequently supplemented by the lens's tunable refraction to yield a sharply focused image on the retina at the rear of the eye. To perform this function, the eye's lens must be able to adjust its refractive power because, unlike the lens of a camera, it is at a fixed distance from the retina. Its refractive power (bulge) is adjustable via a set of ligaments attached at one end to the lens and at another to the internal ciliary muscles. Varying the contraction of the ciliary muscle translates into varying the tension on the ligament, which in turn varies the refractive power of the lens. Should the cornea have a cataract or the lens become cloudy, the retinal image will be blurry, effectively rendering vision blind to spatial details (see upper right panel of Fig. 3.2). In the case of the camera, such poor-quality imaging would result by placing a translucent, cloudy diffuser in front of the lens. Regardless of image quality, the image plane of both the camera and the eye contains light-sensitive chemicals that react differentially to variations of luminance and wavelengths in the image. In the camera, the chemicals are found in a thin layer of the inserted plate or strip of film. In the eye, they are the chemicals, called opsins, contained in special compartments of the photoreceptors.

Much like the black-surfaced shutter mechanism of a camera, the human iris contains a dark pigment, melanin, that absorbs light

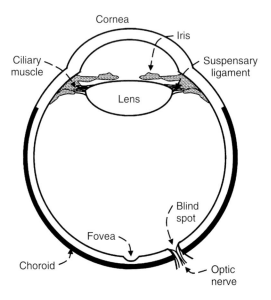

Figure 3.1. The human eye with some of its basic components. See text for details.

and blocks it from entering the eye, except through its adjustable circular hole, the pupil, that acts much like the adjustable aperture in a camera's shutter device. Melanin is also found in a layer of tissue known as the choroid, just behind the photoreceptor segments containing the light-sensitive opsins. Here, melanin absorbs stray light that does not directly activate the opsins in the photoreceptors. Stray light not directed at the receptors' opsin-containing segments can be regarded as "noise." Melanin's absorption of stray light is a case of noise reduction, which thus confers a greater effectiveness of the "signals" carried by the properly directed light rays. A similar principle applies to the camera. Its interior also is covered with a matte black finish for optimal absorption of stray light, that is, light rays not falling directly on the film's surface. Were these light rays to reflect off interior surfaces and eventually land on the film's surface, a loss of photographic image quality would result.

Up to now, despite slight variations, the optics of the camera and eye share much in common. It is after the transduction of light energy into photochemical energy that an immense dissimilarity emerges. Whereas the development and printing of film rely on relatively simple, well-known physical and chemical processes, the sequence of events that occur photochemically in the retina's receptors and that are then projected through cascades of electro-chemical activity to the visual centers in the brain is highly complex and still not adequately understood. While these complex bio-chemical and physiological processes are in principle knowable through application of standard scientific methods (relying as ever on the promise of technical advances), the question of how these processes convert to and register in consciousness poses, according to some, an intractable problem, and according to others, a genuine mystery.

RETINAL BLINDNESSES

It should be clear from the foregoing description that damage to the entire retina or its constituents—the photoreceptors, the intermediate and deep layer neurons and their fibers—can produce massive if not total blindness. Such damage can result from various congenital and hereditary diseases, some of which are present at birth while others are expressed in childhood or early adolescence or in late adulthood. All are serious degenerative diseases that can lead to loss of much if not all of vision. Although inheritance patterns are fairly well understood in many cases, the specific genetic mechanisms contributing to each of the diseases are only now being discovered and explored.

Retinal diseases fall into three categories: *(1)* those diseases that can produce blindness in the central as well as peripheral visual field, *(2)* those that result mainly in peripheral or night blindness (also known as nyctalopia), sparing the central region, and *(3)* those that result mainly in blindness of the central field, sparing the peripheral regions. The following discussion, presenting a partial list of specific diseases within each category, is meant only to illustrate the major types of blindness associated with each category. The interested reader will find a more complete list of retinal diseases in any current ophthalmology text or on any number of reputable websites (e.g., that of the National Eye Institute).

The diseases in the first category commonly result in total or nearly total blindness as the disease progresses and include choroideremia, juvenile retinoschisis, cone-rod dystrophy, and Leber's congenital amaurosis. *Choroideremia* is a rare, inherited disorder that causes progressive loss of vision due to degeneration of the choroid and retina. As the disease progresses, there first is loss of peripheral and nighttime vision, resulting in central "tunnel vision," followed by a loss of central vision. *Juvenile retinoschisis* is an inherited disease diagnosed in childhood that causes progressive loss of central and peripheral vision due to degeneration of the retina. When I was a child in Germany, two of my elementary school classmates, a brother and a sister, were afflicted with this disease. Initially they showed signs of ocular instability and loss of visual function, for which they were prescribed progressively stronger lenses until eventually they were totally blind. *Cone-rod retinal dystrophy* characteristically also leads to impairment of vision early in life. An initial loss of color vision and of visual acuity is followed by night blindness and loss of peripheral visual fields. *Leber's congenital amaurosis*, characterized by defectively developed photoreceptors and subsequent degeneration, results in total or nearly total blindness from birth onward. Here I also list *congenital glaucoma*. Its genetic causes have not been clearly established; symptomatically it is associated (but not invariably) with ocular hypertension produced by the abnormal build up of fluids inside the eye. Initially it produces peripheral and night blindness (see lower right panel of Fig. 3.2) and eventually also causes damage to the optic nerve, which can result in permanent and total loss of vision.

The second category includes the inherited disease *retinitis pigmentosa*, which causes degeneration of mainly the rod photoreceptor cells in the retina. It thus is a progressive form of night blindness, with sparing of the central visual field (see the lower left panel in Fig. 3.2).

In contrast is the third category of retinal disease: *macular degenerations* are often also inheritable retinal pathologies that cause loss of central vision while sparing peripheral vision. However, occasionally they are caused by age-related degenerative processes (see middle left panel in Fig. 3.2). The macula is the central part of the retina containing the fovea and its immediately surrounding perifoveal region. *Stargardt disease* is the most common form of inherited juvenile macular degeneration. Like age-related macular degeneration, it is characterized by a progressive loss of central visual acuity. In late stages of the disease, there may also be noticeable impairment of color vision. Another form of inherited juvenile macular degeneration is *Best disease*, also known as vitelliform macular dystrophy.

Some retinal diseases are secondary to inheritable systemic diseases. For example, diabetes, if not treated, can result in progressive destruction of the network of fine blood vessels found in the retina and can also contribute to retinal detachment and glaucoma, eventually leading to severe blindness. A depiction of an advanced state of diabetic retinopathy is found in the middle right panel of Figure 3.2.

Figure 3.2. View of two young boys. Upper left: By a person with normal vision. Upper right: By a person with mild cataract. Middle left: By a person with macular degeneration. Middle right: By a person with diabetic retinopathy. Lower left: By a person with retinitis pigmentosa. Lower right: By a person with glaucoma.

(Courtesy of the National Eye Institute, National Institutes of Health.)

ALBINISM

Albinism, expressed most noticeably in deficient skin and hair pigmentation, is also an inherited trait accompanied by a functional loss of vision associated with a number of abnormalities. For one, individuals with albinism lack melanin, which as you'll recall is the dark pigment found in the iris and in the choroid layer of the eye. As mentioned, dark pigmentation in both an eye and a camera prevents overexposure of the photosensitive pigments in the receptors or the film. Now imagine a camera whose interior surfaces are covered with a shiny white rather than a matte black finish. Light rays that are not directed by the camera's optical apparatus to the film's light-sensitive layer would reflect off these white interior surfaces, eventually striking the film and thus overexposing it. If you have ever overexposed film by using too large an aperture setting or too long an exposure duration, you know that the resulting photo images are not of very good quality.

The retinal image quality of individuals with albinism, lacking the dark melanin in the choroid layer, suffers from an analogous problem. If you have ever come across such individuals, you might have noticed that some squint their eyes or wear tinted lenses to reduce the amount of light entering their eyes, thus compensating for overexposure to light. They also suffer loss of visual acuity, oculomotor (eye movement) abnormalities that result in involuntary instabilities of eye positions, and less effective stereoptic (stereo depth) vision. These, in turn, may be related to the development of abnormal neural pathways from the retina to the visual areas of the brain. All of these abnormalities contribute to partial blindness, some of which can usually be mitigated with low-vision devices. I recall, for example, an individual with albinism who chaired one of the paper presentation sessions at a vision research conference that I attended some years ago. When introducing the title and authors of each presentation, he would visually scan the conference program by using a magnifying device. Such devices do have their limits, however. On another occasion, while walking across the University of Houston campus, I was about to step into a pedestrian crosswalk just as an SUV that had come to a stop began to pass through the crosswalk. I stepped back just in time and noticed that the driver was a young woman with albinism who was wearing a pair of glasses with a magnifying device mounted on the left lens. Apparently, despite her optical aids, she failed to see me.

RETINAL COLOR BLINDNESS

Our experience of color depends on the psychological attributes of hue, brightness, and saturation. These psychological dimensions correlate (but only approximately) with their respective physically measurable dimensions: wavelength, luminous energy, and purity (the percentage of white light mixed with a single wavelength). Taking into account all three color dimensions, a human with normal color vision is capable of experiencing several million distinct colors. Moreover, the norm for human color vision is trichromacy, so called because it depends on the activation of three distinct types of cone receptors: the S-, M-, and L-cones (S for short wavelength, M for medium wavelength, and L for long wavelength, indicating where in the visible spectrum their respective peak sensitivities lie). The genes regulating the production of the three kinds of cone opsins have been identified.

A common form of visual dysfunction is color blindness. Like hemophilia, it is a sex-linked hereditary defect, being more prevalent in males than females. Several types of color blindness exist. One type is dichromacy, in which one of the three types of cones is defective or missing. There are thus three distinct types of dichromats, depending on which cone type is *lacking*: those with protanopia lack the L-cones; those with deuteranopia lack the M-cones; and those with tritanopia lack the S-cones. None of these individuals can discriminate as many wavelengths in the visible spectrum as those with the full trichromatic complement of cones, and consequently, each experiences fewer color sensations.

A rarer form of hereditary color blindness is monochromacy, which itself falls into three types, depending on which single cone type is *present*. Individuals suffering cone monochromacy are severely color blind, since they are even more deficient in wavelength discrimination and in their range of color experiences than are those afflicted with dichromacy. I noted in the prior chapter that during the day most of us are one up on a nocturnal creature like the tarsier. So, hurrah for us—except for those of us who happen to be the very rare individuals with rod monochromacy and who by genetic misfortune lack cone vision entirely or nearly so. These individuals, besides being severely color blind, also have poor spatial acuity, oculomotor control, and stereoptic vision. The latter two defects, in turn, might be related to a neural reorganization in visual areas of the brain, driven by and partially compensating for the retinal receptor abnormalities. Like individual with albinism, those with rod monochromacy can improve their daytime visual capabilities to some extent by wearing thick tinted glasses: thick, to optically enlarge the retinal image of small objects and to improve their effective visual acuity; and tinted, to reduce, as at night, the overall level of light impinging on their retinae. Nonetheless, during the day they will permanently fail to see many types of visual objects and experience far fewer of their perceptual qualities than most of us do.

Color blindness, like other forms of partial blindness, is actually a relative term. In humans we gauge color blindness against the norm, trichromacy. While the dichromatic vision of some creatures like the dog is color-blind relative to human trichromacy, trichromatic vision is color blind relative to the tetrachromatic vision found among some species of fish, amphibians, and reptiles (and, according to reports from Cambridge University in England, a woman who might have a genetic mutation that bestows her with tetrachromatic vision), and the pentachromatic vision found among some species of birds. Presumably tetrachromatic vision (of, for example, the pigeon and trout, both of whom have, in addition to the L-, M-, and S-cones, receptors sensitive to ultraviolet light) can discriminate among more wavelengths than can human trichromatic vision, and pentachromatic vision, in turn, can discriminate among still more wavelengths. Just as it is hard for a human with dichromatic or monochromatic vision to imagine the nuances of trichromatic color vision, it is hard for us to imagine the qualitative subtlety and sumptuousness of our color experiences if we all had tetrachromatic or pentachromatic vision. We can surmise, however, that our perceptual experience would have available to it a richer, more nuanced color palette.

NATURE VERSUS NURTURE?

Although the anatomical and physiological foundations for some basic visual abilities and disabilities are inherited, the postnatal development of any abilities present at birth as well as the acquisition of additional ones are influenced by environmental variables. For example, the development of sophisticated skills, such as the recognition of facial expressions, must take advantage of basic visual processes that, though present in rough form at birth, must be molded and refined by exposure to an adequately rich environment. For that reason, the development of normal space and object perception in adulthood presupposes both a normal visual system at birth and a normal (natural and cultural) visual environment during infancy and early childhood. In line with this, extensive research conducted since the 1960s indicates that it is not a matter of nature *versus* nurture; instead, the cooperative and interactive roles of nature *and* nurture are instrumental in normal postnatal development of visual functions. These cooperative and interactive roles are sometimes subverted, however. If especially early on in life the input to the visual system from the environment is blocked or degraded due to, say, a congenital condition or an impoverished environment, permanent visual deficits may persist throughout adulthood.

Studies have shown that in some organisms (e.g., cats) the postbirth maturation of visual capabilities, such as depth perception, can proceed with or without exposure to a visual environment. It is as though in some species the very young newborn is a fetus ex utero, still developing along a genetically and epigenetically drawn growth curve not subject to vagaries of the visual environment. Although such maturational processes also play important roles in human postnatal visual development of, for example, the discrimination of yellow from blue objects and of depth perception, other visual abilities such as red–green color discrimination, luminance discrimination, and motion detection exist at birth. However, at birth or shortly thereafter, human visual capabilities are usually of a rudimentary kind, and even if genetically "preprogrammed" (nature), they still require plenty of environmental input (nurture) for their maintenance, augmentation, and sharpening or fine tuning. Examples are the abilities to discriminate among objects and to resolve spatial details or orientation differences. In fact, the nature–nurture *pas de deux* has been demonstrated in studies showing that the visual brain can, to some extent, be functionally "rewired" under certain types, and during specific periods, of environmentally manipulated postbirth development. Moreover, the visual brain can be rewired in such ways as to suppress the development of visual capabilities occurring under normal nonlaboratory conditions.

For ethical reasons, such studies were conducted experimentally only on the visual systems of animals like cats or monkeys, which can serve as models of human vision. Related human research can be conducted; however, it relies on "experimental treatments" performed by nature, about which I'll say more shortly.

What about other, more complicated visual skills, like reading, that typically require a prolonged period of training? Since written language is a cultural artifact rather than a natural, instinctive signal system, one might readily reason that the transmission and acquisition of reading skills, usually through formal education, also square with culture or nurture rather than with nature. Taking after behaviorist B. F. Skinner and his forerunner James Watson, many people whom I would call environmental optimists or meliorists tend to align along the nurture pole of the nature–nurture axis. "Give me a poor infant boy, and I'll make of him a prince instead of a pauper" is their progressive battle cry. But what if the boy is born with dyslexia? Will the dyslexic prince learn to read—to see words—as readily or easily as the nondyslexic pauper? Not likely, since causal factors contributing to developmental dyslexia—in former times also called congenital word blindness—have a high genetic loading. There are biological, natural limits to the human spirit, even one as creatively exuberant as that of the sculptor Auguste Rodin, a severe dyslexic.

Given a normal visual system, one's visual skills are no doubt sharpened by practice, also known as perceptual learning. A trained radiologist clearly can detect in an X-ray subtle patterns that most of us cannot see. Or is it that we can see them but simply cannot interpret them or understand their significance? Based on recent research in vision science, I believe that with practice one can acquire templates (sometimes called adaptive filters) that allow one to make finer and finer perceptual discriminations and therefore to notice small pattern differences that are not apparent to the untrained viewer. But even here, as in most other skills, the gift of natural talent may also play a role. It would be interesting to see what visual skills among radiologists with the same level of experience and training differentiate the best from the worst and to what extent these skills are biologically inheritable.

CONGENITAL CATARACTS AND MOTES IN THEORISTS' EYES

Imagine you are a sanguine environmentalist or a faithful empiricist according to whom all or nearly all visual capabilities are absent at birth and acquired only after some experience in a visual environment. John Locke, the 17th–18th century British thinker, was for reasons philosophical and political an empiricist. He ceded few human abilities to any God-granted favor, including the ability to rule England. In his revision of *An Essay Concerning Human Understanding*, Locke published a letter from his Irish colleague William Molyneux, who posed the following *Gedanken* (thought) experiment:

> Suppose a man *born* blind, and now adult, and taught by his *touch* to distinguish between a cube and a sphere of the same metal, and nighly of the same bigness, so as to tell, when he felt one and the other, which is the cube, which the sphere. Suppose then the cube and sphere placed on a table, and the blind man be made to see: *query*, whether *by his sight, before he touched them* he could now distinguish and tell which is the globe, which the cube?

Molyneux's answer, with which Locke concurred, was "No." To justify their answer, they assumed that the solid objects (a) would at first appear as flat or two-dimensional and thus (b) would not be recognizable as solid objects by one with untutored sight. They argued further that (c) such recognition would, however, occur through some sort of associative binding of tactual/kinesthetic and visual "ideas" once the formerly blind man had opportunities to simultaneously view, manipulate, and touch them. Afterward he would be able to recognize the 3-D shape of the object by sight alone.

Congenital cataracts, resulting from cloudiness of the lenses, and opacities of the cornea usually produce partial rather than total blindness. You can mimic this effect by placing milk glass, a half of a ping pong ball, or a piece of a plastic shopping bag over each of your eyes. Some light will pass through the translucent obstruction. When I place a single layer of plastic over my eyes and visually scan my office by moving my head, I experience a very blurred and much flattened world and can make out the two-dimensional (2-D) shape and the color of large objects as I approach them. When I double the plastic sheet in front of my eyes, I am still able to distinguish the large depthless areas of lightness corresponding to my windows and the darker areas corresponding to my dark gray filing cabinets, but my laptop computer is not even a dark blur, and I must approach much closer to such objects to make out their 2-D shapes or colors. A still severer form of vision loss occurs when I lightly close my eyelids and look at the bright light fixtures over my head. After a brief period during which afterimages fade from my mind, my vision is of a more or less uniform red field, since the light is filtered through the red tissue of the lids. And while I can vaguely detect the motion of my arm moving left to right or up to down between my eyes and the light source, it is hard for me to make out anything about the shape of these fleeting shadowy ghosts.

Congenital cataracts and corneal opacities are examples of nature's (mal-) experiments that I mentioned in passing above. If these conditions are not corrected sufficiently early through surgery, the affected individuals will be blind to patterns, 2-D and 3-D shapes, and colors throughout their lives. After surgery, these individuals might, to some, serve as case studies yielding rare empirical evidence in response to the query posed in Molyneux's *Gedanken* experiment. For example, according to the reports of psychobiologist Austin Riesen, some school-age children who had cataracts surgically removed (presumably sufficiently early in their life) were able to report brightness and color differences shortly after the operation. They could also discriminate simple geometric patterns but remained deficient in identifying more complex forms or objects: They could identify specific details or features in these objects but could not perceive them as a whole.

At least one adult case study, reported in 1962 by psychologists Richard Gregory and Jean Wallace in England, compared the pre- and postoperative vision of a middle-aged individual rendered partially blind from infancy by a corneal opacity. It turned out to be a rather sad, if not tragic, case. Whereas preoperatively the individual had been socially and occupationally functional and had enjoyed a sense of competence and accomplishment *despite* his visual impairment, postoperatively he suffered a sense of incompetence, some social opprobrium, and a loss of self-esteem *because* his vision, though somewhat improved, remained poor and he still could not see as well as his peers. Other cases have reported similar results, with the affected individuals suffering grief, depression, and a sense of loss, once they realized through their somewhat improved vision what might have been, but was not and will not be.

Nonetheless, from a scientific and philosophic viewpoint, these cases have contributed to the study and theory of perceptual development and learning. Despite the personal travails of the patients, their vision usually did improve slowly during the post-operative period. And in the case reported by Gregory and Wallace and no doubt to the posthumous delight of Messrs. Locke and Molyneux, the individual's restored vision was often "educated" by his senses of touch and hearing. This case seemed to confirm one prominent approach to perceptual development proposed near the middle of the 20th century, which advanced the theory that post-birth vision developed slowly and laboriously and that eye movements played a key role in this process. However, as noted by Gregory and Wallace, that theory—and in my opinion Locke's and Molyneux's theoretical answer to their *Gedanken* experiment—rested implicitly on the assumption that the acquisition of visual functions by an adult whose sight was restored was indicative of the normal postnatal acquisition of similar visual functions. After all, according to a strict empiricist assumption, what relates the neonate to the blind adult is that both, having few if any visual abilities, must acquire them through extensive visual experience. Hence, postoperative acquisition of visual function in previously blind adults should resemble the normal postnatal acquisition of infants.

This assumption turns out to be the mote in the empiricist's eye inspecting this issue. As described shortly, the adult visual system is far less modifiable by environmental inputs than an infant's immature one is. Therefore, extrapolating from the laborious touch- and hearing-aided acquisition of visual function in, say, adults whose congenital cataracts have been surgically removed to acquisition of similar visual functions during postnatal development is not warranted. Effects of extensive exposure to the visual environment in a formerly blind adult simply are no match for the effects of the same exposure during infancy. Nature contributes tremendously to the acquisition of visual function by imposing severe restrictions on when in life such exposure is maximally effective. Moreover, the *inherited nature* of the visual system at birth is such that various rudimentary visual functions such as the direction of motion, brightness, and wavelength can be discriminated at birth while other functions are highly and rapidly acquirable shortly thereafter. In view of the important contribution of nature to the inherited structure and plasticity of the human visual system, the larger philosophic beam in Locke's and Molyneux's eyes was a radical empiricism that yielded little if anything to nature not only in adulthood but also at birth.

We know now, more than 300 years after Molyneux posed his *Gedanken* experiment, that the development of many visual functions in nonhuman primates proceed at an amazingly rapid pace after birth. This rapid development rests on built-in anatomical and physiological properties that provide the neonatal visual system with an articulated functional architecture at or very shortly after birth. Although the pace of development may be somewhat slower in humans, there is no reason to believe that similar built-in "givens" are not in place in the human neonate. These givens are nevertheless highly "plastic" or modifiable by experience, particularly during what are called critical developmental periods, that is, postbirth periods during which the development of the functional wiring of the brain is particularly sensitive to visual environmental influences. Prior to and after these periods, the visual environment exerts a much weaker influence, hence the laboriously acquired visual functions of individuals who had their congenital cataracts removed late in life. It is for this reason that interventions used to overcome certain congenital visual defects must be administered prior to or early on during such critical periods—ideally within a few months of birth—in order to obtain lasting beneficial effects. A couple of examples follow.

FORM AND STEREOBLINDNESS

A typical patient or experimental subject showing up at the University of Houston's School of Optometry is a person with congenital amblyopia, a condition affecting about 2%–4% of children and sometimes also called "lazy eye." It manifests itself in one of two ways. First, in anisometropic amblyopia, one of the eyes, due to some structural or optical flaw (e.g., a congenital cataract), provides a highly blurred retinal image relative to the other eye. Here, because of a major loss of visual acuity, individuals have severe difficulties making out an object's identity and location when it is viewed by the amblyopic eye. Second, in strabismic amblyopia, the optic axis of the amblyopic eye is noticeably misaligned relative to that of the normal eye and appears turned inward or outward. In both types of amblyopia, the two eyes provide highly discordant information about the world to the higher visual centers in the brain. We know from experimental studies performed on cats and monkeys that cortical binocular neurons (neurons in the visual centers of the brain that can respond to input from both eyes) (a) are quite plentiful at or shortly after birth and (b) lose their binocularity when highly discordant images are projected on the two retinae after birth. To compensate for this problem, the neural connections from the healthy eye to the immature binocular neurons compete during critical postbirth periods of development with the connections from the defective eye. The winner turns out to be the connections from the healthy eye, with input from the unhealthy eye being suppressed, having little effect on the now "rewired" monocularly driven cortical neurons. As a result, not only visual acuity but also form discrimination, pattern recognition, and some other visual functions are greatly compromised in the defective eye as compared to the healthy eye.

Another consequence is that such neurons can no longer process the slightly discordant images falling on the two eyes, often even when, as in patients suffering from strabismic amblyopia, the defective eye's alignment has been corrected surgically. In normal vision, such slight interocular image disparities provide the input to the binocular part of the brain for "computation" of binocular (stereoptic) depth. That means that, if you do not have amblyopia, you would be able to experience artificially produced stereoptic depth phenomena such as 3-D movies, slides

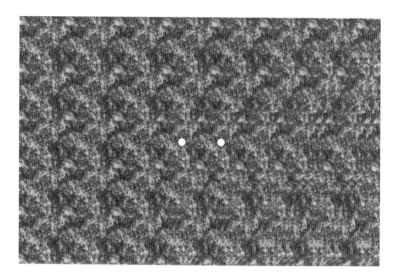

Figure 3.3. Example of an autostereogram. By diverging or converging, your eyes try to fuse the two white dots in the middle of the display into a single binocular image (when this happens you will probably see three dots: a central fused dot flanked symmetrically by two diplopic or "double-image" dots). Depending on whether you diverge or converge your eyes, you should eventually see a horse in front of a background or a horse-shaped cutout in the background. For people not familiar with these types of displays, seeing the horses in depth may require persistent attempts and practice. (Reproduced with permission from Bachmann et al., 2007.)

viewed through stereoscopes, and the variety of published "magic-eye" autostereograms that, when viewed with the eyes slightly crossed inward or diverged outward, eventually yield an impression of an object in depth (see Fig. 3.3).

It turns out that persons with amblyopia whose ocular problems are not corrected sufficiently early in life (i.e., before or during the postbirth critical period for development of normal binocular vision) are permanently stereoblind. They cannot see stereoptic depth phenomena such as these "magic-eye" objects no matter how long they look at them or how hard they cross or diverge their eyes. I have come across several such individuals in the course on visual perception that I teach. I have also known one student whose "lazy (strabismic) eye" was surgically corrected shortly after her first birthday, and she is able to see most (but not all) such magic-eye images. The reason is that the critical period for development of binocular vision in humans starts at about 2–3 months and lasts for about 4 years after birth. Her corrective operation very likely occurred shortly after the start of the critical period, and thus her resulting corrected vision allowed her binocular cortical system to receive normal binocular input for the remainder of the critical period. If she had had her corrective surgery performed before the onset of the critical period, she might well have been able to see all such images. On the other hand, had the surgery been performed later in the critical period, she would have preserved less of her binocular vision. And if the surgery had occurred after she was 4 years of age, it would have had merely a cosmetic effect: her eyes would look normal, but she would not be able to see stereodepth at all.

Fortunately the visual system has several "back-up" subsystems that can make use of monocular information to yield perception of depth. To illustrate this point, I recall reading a newspaper column a few years ago that described a wide receiver on a professional football team whose ability to catch a pass was excellent despite his having only monocular vision due to the loss of one eye. I suspect that if his left eye was lost, he most likely was a left wide receiver, since, while running down the left flank of the field, he would, by turning his head to the right, have immediate use of his right eye to see the oncoming passed football.

The types of visual blindness discussed in this chapter arise from hereditary and congenital flaws that disrupt the influence of normally adequate environmental inputs on the development of the immature visual functions present at birth. However, even a healthy neonate *receiving* adequate visual inputs can develop visual deficits if the child does not or cannot *actively and selectively control* these inputs. Moreover, in adults, nonvisual environmental factors such as nutritional deficiencies or deficits acquired due to damage to the visual areas of the brain can produce temporary or permanent visual deficits. So even if the visual system and the visual environment are or have been normal, visual deficits can be acquired in one way or another. The next chapter deals with the types of blindness resulting from some of these deficits.

FOUR

OUR MISFORTUNE

Blindness 2

Vision is part gift and part accomplishment. Happily, if biology has done its part, most of us are endowed at birth with well-structured and well-functioning, albeit immature, visual systems, whose postnatal maturation puts inevitable finishing touches on processes initiated prenatally. The postnatal environment of each individual infant must promote not only the maintenance and fine-tuning of endowed visual abilities but also the acquisition, maintenance, and fine-tuning of new ones. And since some of these new visual skills, for example, landing a space shuttle safely, depend on the prior development of more basic ones, like the ability to visually discriminate distances and the speeds and directions of motion, it is clear that the accumulation of sophisticated visual skills, important even for more mundane occupations, is somewhat like building one sound foundation upon another. As we saw in the previous chapter, should the postnatal visual environment not play its supportive role, some severe and long-lasting visual disabilities can result. And even if development proceeds in the best of environments, resulting in a normal, mature visual system, the vagaries of fortune, especially accident and disease, can also lead to noticeable visual dysfunction.

DEVELOPMENTAL INATTENTIONAL BLINDNESS?

An important function of vision is to control and guide action or behavior, but the converse is also true: action and behavior helps to shape vision. It is for this reason that normal exposure to opportunities for visuomotor coordination is of prime importance. A host of studies have shown that in higher mammals the normal development of visual skills depends on the organism's ability to establish a sensory-motor correlation between self-initiated movement and consequent changes of visual stimulation. These movements can be as simple as the saccades that allow us to change our eyes' fixation from one word to another as we read or as complex as the coordinated and simultaneous movements of the eyes, head, trunk, and limbs as we approach to inspect the markings on a butterfly's wings. If these opportunities to establish visuomotor correlations through active visual exploration are not available during early development, the subsequent deficit in pattern discrimination abilities can be as severe as that produced by total deprivation of light.

Humans, like other higher mammals, are born with innate orienting responses to salient stimuli in or entering into the visual field. These orienting mechanisms can be regarded as expressions of an exogenous, stimulus-driven attention that is rather passive and obligatory, in the sense that salient stimuli "capture" this attention. Nonetheless, in early infancy it serves as a foundation on which rests the subsequent development of another type of orienting attention that is voluntary and selective, in the sense that the organism endogenously initiates the shift of attention toward selected stimuli and thus "captures" them for further visual analysis. The acquisition of this latter, voluntary attention depends crucially on opportunities for *self-initiated, active* visual exploration, as shown by many studies in which such attention does not develop properly if an organism is passively transported through the visual environment. Without this voluntary attentional skill, the ability to discriminate among visual *feature* *"primitives"* such as brightness or orientation is preserved; however, the ability to discriminate among the rich variety of more complex patterns formed by distinctive conjunctions of primitives, called *conjunctive features*, is greatly impaired.

For instance, young kittens and chimpanzees reared in an environment that restricts their opportunities for active visual exploration can discriminate nearly as well as normally reared animals among different levels of brightness (● vs. ●) or orientation (≡ vs. |||), but they are greatly impaired in discriminating Δ from ∇ or $\perp$ from $\top$. The latter patterns share the same simple orientation primitives (horizontal and obliques or horizontal and verticals) but not the higher-order relational features (vertices or corners) made of distinctive conjunctions of these simple features. Learning such conjunctive feature distinctions requires the deployment of selective attention, a skill which the animals reared restrictively fail to develop.

Despite the problems of extrapolating information from animal studies to explain human behavior, I'll venture to say that many infants raised in an orphanage (or, sadly, by uncaring parents) where, except for feeding, they are mostly neglected and confined to their tiny cribs, with minimal opportunity to actively explore their minimally furnished environment, might later, as young children, have difficulty with recognizing (i.e., might remain blind to) the distinctions between **t** and **f**, **g** and **q**, **n** and **h**, and so on.

They would lack the foundational pattern discrimination skills for acquiring the still more sophisticated skill of reading, which, in turn, is a foundational skill for proper schooling, which, in turn, is foundational for a skilled occupation, and so on.

DIETARY BLINDNESS

Even if we are blessed with caring parents and a stimulating environment during infancy and childhood, uncontrollable environmental factors can cause or promote visual deficits in an otherwise healthy visual system. Imagine the following. It is March of 1797. You are a settler living in the subarctic wilds near Hudson Bay in present day Quebec, Canada. Your crop of winter squash was nipped in the bud by the early onset of the harshest winter you have yet experienced. It lingers into spring, by which time you have depleted your larder's store of dried halibut and Arctic cod. For some time your dietary mainstay has been nothing but the wild rice and the dwindling rations of dry beans you purchased late last fall. Although high in carbohydrates, protein, and several of the B vitamins, these foods do not support your dietary needs for Vitamin A. You have noticed some minor visual problems during your daytime activities; however, at night, your vision has deteriorated dramatically to the point where you do not dare to leave the immediate vicinity of your dwelling. You are wondering whether or not you are suffering from some kind malady that will leave your vision permanently impaired. By July, after you have feasted on plenty of fish harvested from the bay and on ripe berries gathered in the wild, you are relieved to find your vision has returned to normal. Although you could not have known it, you were suffering from *avitaminotic nyctalopia*, a type of night blindness, during the prior winter. It was caused by a prolonged (but fortunately temporary) vitamin A deficiency in your diet.

Vitamin A is known to play an important role in the regeneration of the rod photopigment, rhodopsin. Rhodopsin molecules are "bleached" when they react with photons of light, rendering them inert to further stimulation by light. If, due to a chronic dietary Vitamin A deficiency, bleached rhodopsin molecules are not restored to their prior unbleached photoreactive state, nocturnal vision eventually deteriorates to dysfunctional levels. Epidemics of such night blindness have been known to occur in regions where the availability of plants or animal food sources containing vitamin A was drastically reduced. For example, it has been common in parts of Southeast Asia where rice is the staple food. Fortunately, avitaminotic nyctalopia can be readily treated by increasing dietary vitamin A.

However, dietary night blindness can occur even when food sources rich in vitamin A are plentiful. Imagine the next sad scenario. You have been a closet alcoholic for a several years. Besides the spider angianomas that give the tip of your nose a ruddy and friendly glow, you recently have noticed an increase of fatigue, an intolerable itch has been building up in your torso and arms, and you no longer wear your favorite pair of boots due to the swelling of your ankles and lower legs. In addition, you have noticed that you have difficulty driving at night—even when you are sober. Troubled, you go to your doctor and are diagnosed with cirrhosis of the liver. What you did not know is that vitamin A deficiencies can result from this disease, as well as from other liver diseases such as hepatitis, and that night blindness can be a symptom of it. Like avitaminotic night blindness, it too can be treated. However, since the effects of cirrhosis are not reversible, you must treat your night blindness with (massive) daily doses of vitamin A to compensate for the permanent loss of normal liver function, recalling with regret a wise saying you read years ago: Rum makes for a great servant, but a bad master.

BRIEF INTERLUDE I. PSYCHOGENIC BLINDNESS?

All of the blindnesses discussed up to now can be traced back to physical or biological causes. However, it is claimed that some blindnesses for which no organic cause can be determined are psychogenic. In the heyday of psychodynamic theories of personality and its dysfunctions, Sigmund Freud attributed such blindnesses to hysterical neuroses, theorizing that they were merely the physical manifestations of deep psychological, or more usually psychosexual, distress. Apparently, 19th century, *fin de siècle* Vienna, where Freud practiced his psychoanalytical techniques, was rife with sexually repressed young women who comprised the majority of his patients with symptoms of hysteria. By psychodynamic accounts, a memory of a severe psychological (sexual) trauma, an undesirable (aggressive or again sexual) drive, or a dangerous (homicidal or yet again sexual) impulse can present a threat so strong to a patient's conscious ego that she cannot simply repress into her unconscious mind her anxiety about this threat. Instead, she converts her intensely painful anxiety into symptoms that guard against it. One way to do so is to psychologically shut the gateways to the ego, namely, by anesthetizing the senses. If vision happens to be the sense *de jour*, we have a case of *hysterical blindness*.

I am no fan of Freudian psychodynamics—and yet. . . . Some years ago, a crisis produced by a noxious mix of personal and career concerns was building up in my life. Feeling chronically stressed and anxiety ridden, I experienced an intense panic attack one evening, in a social setting with acquaintances over wine and other drinks. One of the manifestations of this attack was something that I can only describe as a perforation and subsequent complete blanking of my visual field, akin to what happens on a cinema screen when the film in the projector overheats and melts. Hoping and praying that my hearing would be spared so that

I could mask my blindness by maintaining conversation with my friends, I gutted out the next few minutes. Fortunately my hearing did not fade; and, lo, my vision began to recover in fragments—much like its fading, but in reverse—until my visual field was fully restored. Since then, I happily have been spared any repetitions of this experience. I don't know if this attack was a case of hysterical blindness, but I do believe that intense physical or psychological stress might contribute to at least a temporary blindness.

BRIEF INTERLUDE II. THE FUNCTIONAL ARCHITECTURE OF THE VISUAL BRAIN (AND SOME BASIC CONSEQUENCES OF ITS DISRUPTION)

Before we return to discussion of blindnesses having an organic etiology, we should examine some basics in the neuroanatomy and neurophysiology underlying vision. Seeing the world around us starts with processes occurring in the retinae of the eyes. During embryonic differentiation, the retinae emanate from the same tissue that eventually becomes the visual brain, and together, they comprise the neuroanatomy of the visual system, with the brain extending all the way down to (or up from) the retinae. To understand some of the important neural underpinnings of vision, we need briefly to discuss the functional architecture of the brain (i.e., the structure of the visual system as it relates to its function). This will allow us also to understand how seeing malfunctions when neural damage is done to the visual system.

With these notions in mind, let's turn to Figure 4.1, a schematic of how the visual world projects onto the retinae of the two eyes and how from there the information contained in these projected images, once they are transformed into the electrochemical energy of the

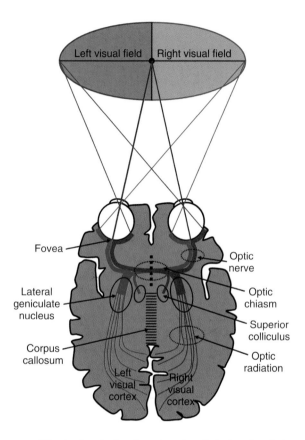

Figure 4.1. The visual projections from the retina, via the lateral geniculate nucleus, to the primary visual cortex and to the superior colliculus of the midbrain. The left and right visual hemifields project, respectively, to the right and left primary visual cortices, which communicate via the corpus callosum.

nervous system by the photoreceptors, is transmitted via nerve fibers to different areas of the brain. The neural messages generated in the retinae exit the eyes through their optic nerves, each a bundle of about one million nerve fibers. The optic nerves from the two eyes partially cross at the optic chiasm, and project from there mainly—about 90% of the fibers—to the left and right lateral geniculate bodies located in brain region known as the thalamus; the remainder of the optic nerve fibers project to the left and right superior colliculi located in a region known as the midbrain. From the lateral geniculate bodies, a vast majority of the neural messages in turn project via what are called optic radiation fibers to the respective left and right primary visual cortices, each also known as area V1. An important aspect of this anatomical design is that any stimulus in the left visual hemifield (all of the area in the visual field to the left of vertical meridian passing through the fixation point, designated by the black dot) projects to the right hemiretinae of both eyes, and from there the contents of the stimulus, transduced by the photoreceptors into the neural signature of the nervous system, projects via the right lateral geniculate nucleus (and less so via the right superior colliculus) to the right visual brain. Conversely, stimuli in the right visual hemifield similarly end up being processed in the left visual brain. The two sides of the brain—the left and right hemispheres—can communicate with each other through the approximately 250 million nerve fibers comprising a structure known as the corpus callosum.

In V1, the primary visual cortex, and at subsequent, secondary (or "higher") areas—such as V2, V3, and so forth—of the visual cortex that directly or via a series of cascading stages receive input from area V1, the neural processing encodes specific features such as the spatial location, shape, lightness, color, direction of motion, depth, and texture of visual objects. This encoding process actually starts in the retinae and proceeds with increasingly higher specificity as the neural messages progress through the central visual system. Details of these processes and their interactions at cortical levels are highly complex and beyond the purview of this book. For that reason, Figure 4.2 renders a highly condensed representation of some of the interesting characteristics of cortical organization. One such aspect is that the

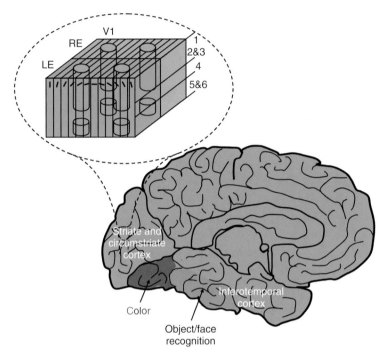

Figure 4.2. Top: A schematic of the columnar organization of V1, proceeding from its top layer 1 down to its bottom layer 6, with different columnar slabs of neurons responding selectively to different line or edge orientations and "blob" (orange cylindrical) areas responding to chromatic properties of a stimulus. Left-eye input is designated in green, right-eye input in blue. This columnar organization repeats itself in modular fashion to cover the entire binocular visual field. Bottom: Areas of the visual cortex that have specialized functions.

visual world is initially processed in V1 by neural "modules" that respond to specific features of perceived stimuli, such as line or edge orientation, wavelength, spatial location, and motion. The outputs from these feature modules are then routed to cortical areas or regions located at later stages of processing, with each of these regions specialized to process specific attributes of visual stimuli. Figure 4.2 also shows where in the cortical visual system some of these attributes, such as color, static form, dynamic form, facial recognition, motion, depth, and so forth, are processed. Each of the modules at earlier levels and the specific areas at later levels are analogous to "parallel processors" in present-day desktop computers, in which each processor performs a particular function in the overall computational system. Indeed, many visual scientists often refer to the neural processes in the brain as expressions of its "computational" strategies and functions.

Let's follow this analogy a bit further. If a computer engineer were to monitor the activity of the parallel processors in a desktop computer, he or she would notice that the electrical circuitry of a particular processor, for example, one responsible for word processing, would be active when in use for a task, for example, preparing the manuscript for this book, while the circuitry of another processor, for example, the one handling e-mail messages, is not active. Similarly, using current techniques such as functional magnetic resonance imaging (fMRI) to monitor brain activity, a neuroscientist finds that when an observer looks at a static multicolored scene, his or her brain's "color processor" is active while its "motion processor" is inactive. Examples of such area-specific dissociations between the cortical processing of color and motion are shown in Figure 4.3. Moreover, if a processor in a computer is faulty or disabled, a particular program, for example, word processing, will malfunction or be disabled. Similarly, if one of the specialized areas of the visual brain is faulty or disabled due to a partial or total lesion, a particular visual function, for example, color processing, will be partially or totally disabled.

More globally the cortical visual system consists of two separate pathways, the dorsal and the ventral pathway, along which signals originating in V1 are routed. Schematically, as shown in Figure 4.4, the ventral cortical pathway originates in V1 primarily in a class of neurons called *parvocellular* (P), proceeds to V2, then to V4, and then

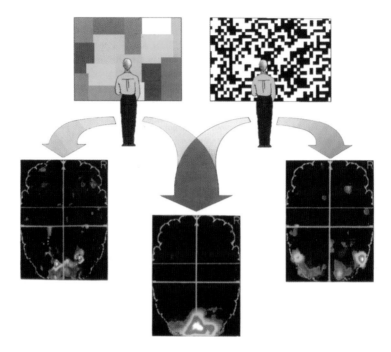

Figure 4.3. Brain images showing area-specific activations (left) of the visual cortical color centers (V4), (right) of the motion centers (V5), and (center) of nonspecific activation of primary visual cortex (V1).
(Reproduced with permission from Zeki, 1999.)

to the inferotemporal (IT) cortex. Neuroscientists have given this pathway various names to suggest the functional roles it plays. Mortimer Mishkin and Leslie Ungerleider, for example, have called it the *what* or the *object* pathway because it is deemed essential for the analysis and identification of objects. David Milner and Melvyn Goodale refer to it as the *vision-for-perception* pathway, because it is crucial for the *conscious* recognition and identification of visual objects. Correct object identification depends on the processing of

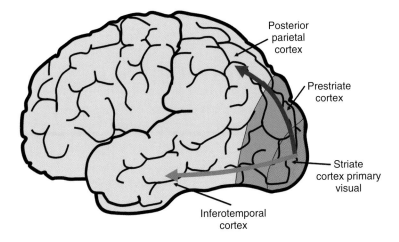

Figure 4.4. The ventral (blue arrow) and dorsal (red arrow) streams of cortical visual processing.

shape, contour, and color in this pathway. For instance, a tomato and a banana clearly have a different shape and could be discriminated and identified on that basis alone. However, a green and a yellow banana are different objects because they do not provide the same affordances to, say, a monkey in the jungle canopy. The latter is tasty and edible; the former is not. Similarly, humans generally allow green tomatoes to ripen to a red color before eating them.

The dorsal pathway also originates in V_1 primarily in another class of neurons called magnocellular (M), proceeds via V_2 to V_3, then to area V_5 (also known as area MT), and thence to the parietal lobe. This pathway, based on the putative visual functions it supports, has been named the *where* or *spatial* pathway by Ungerleider and Mishkin and the *vision-for-action* pathway by Goodale and Milner. It is crucial for determining the spatial properties of an object such as its location in, or motion through, visual space, and its spatial orientation and size. In order for the monkey in the canopy to eat a ripe banana, it must know where the banana is located in its visual space and how to reach for it, and similarly for a human reaching into a vegetable bin and grabbing a ripe tomato. The superior colliculus, located in the midbrain, can be considered a part of the where or spatial pathway, since it is important for directing one's center of gaze, via eye movements, to the locations of various objects in the visual field.

By now you can begin to understand how neural damage to different parts of the visual system can cause deficits in correspondingly different visual functions. Sometimes the neurological damage, as in the precise surgical sectioning of the corpus callosum (performed, for example, in rare cases to treat severe and intractable epilepsy), can lead to predictably specific losses of visual function. More often, however, an unforeseeable event such as a stroke, malignant growth, carbon monoxide poisoning, or closed head injury causes more diffuse damage. Medical reports of such cases have been published at least since the middle of the 19th century. In them, one typically finds that a deficit of a particular visual function (e.g., reading words) is associated with deficits of other functions (e.g., object and face recognition), although on rare occasions a highly specific or "pure" deficit presents itself. Regardless of the extent of visual damage in these various cases, they go a long way toward elucidating the neural substrates of visual perception.

THE BRAIN'S BANES I. DISCONNECTION SYNDROMES AND BLINDSIGHT

Let's now look at some blindnesses that could result from neurological damage. Inspecting Figure 4.1, we can see that a partial or complete sectioning of the left eye's optic nerve between the eye and the optic chiasm would render the left eye partially or completely blind. This is an example of a disconnection syndrome, since the retinally generated neural signals can no longer be transmitted to subsequent, brain levels of visual processing. The affected person would, of course, still have full sight through the right eye. However, depending on the extent of the disconnection, his or her vision is only partially or not at all binocular. Since stereo depth perception depends on binocular inputs to the visual cortex, this person would be partially or totally stereoblind. Consider now that the fibers in the nerve bundle between the chiasm and the left lateral geniculate body are partially or fully sectioned. Here, the affected person would be partially or totally blind in the right visual hemifield (i.e., blind to stimuli falling to the right of fixation).

A few actual case studies will further illustrate some of the partial blindnesses resulting from specific neurological disconnections in the visual system. In the 1970s, neurophysiologists Colin Blakemore and Donald Mitchell at Cambridge University reported on a young man who as a child fell from his bicycle, landing headfirst with such force that his optic chiasm was completely severed along the vertical dashed line shown in Figure 4.1. What were the consequences of this damage? As long as both eyes were open, he had vision in the whole visual field—but only partially so, as it turns out. Normally, when only one eye is open we have vision both in the left and right visual hemifields, that is, both to the left and right of fixation. However, careful study of Figure 4.1 ought to convince you that the young man with a sectioned optic chiasm was blind in the left visual field when only his left eye was open and blind in his right visual field when only his right eye was open. The man suffered from partial stereoblindness in that he was not able to achieve stereoptic depth discrimination of a large part of his visual field due to his having lost binocular cortical input from both eyes.

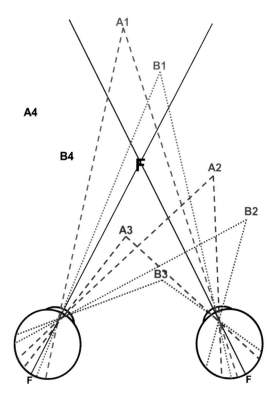

Figure 4.5. A schematic of binocular-depth space. Here, both eyes fixate on the point F, which projects onto the fovea, small F, of each eye. The optic axes of the two eyes, depicted by the two solid lines, intersect at F and form four sectors of the depth space.

To analyze this circumstance further, Figure 4.5 depicts two eyes fixating on a point, F. The optical axes of the two eyes are designated by the two solid lines which intersect at F. This way of diagramming the visual field allows us to schematically divide it up into four pielike sectors, designated by the numbers 1–4. If we consider two depth-separated objects, A1 and B1, both in Section 1 and more distant than F, we note that their images project onto the nasal hemiretinae (the halves of the retinae nearer to the nose) of the two eyes. Due to the specific sectioning that occurred in the young man's optic chiasm, the neural signals from the two nasal hemiretinae cannot reach his visual brain. Consequently, they cannot interact binocularly at the cortical level, thus rendering him stereoblind with respect to A1 and B1, and all other objects in Sector 1. Now consider the two stimuli, A2 and B2, in Sector 2. While both project images to the temporal hemiretina of the left eye, they also project images to the nasal hemiretina of the right eye. While the neural signals from the left eye do project to the left visual cortex, those from the right eye cannot. Consequently, there again can be no binocular interaction at the cortical level. Hence, the young man is stereoblind with respect to A2 and B2, and all other objects in Sector 2. Without including the corresponding projection lines, a similar conclusion holds for the depicted objects A4 and B4, and all other objects in Sector 4. This leaves Sector 3 for consideration. Note that here objects A3 and B3 both project their images to the temporal hemiretina of both eyes. Since the neural signals generated in the temporal hemiretinae proceed unimpaired to the visual cortex, they can there interact binocularly via the corpus callosum to produce stereoptic depth discrimination of A3 from B3, and of all other objects falling in Sector 3. The net result is that the individual's ability to discriminate depth on the basis of stereoptic vision is limited to Sector 3. Had he additionally suffered from a severed corpus callosum, he would, of course, be stereoblind in the entire visual field. Blakemore and Michell also studied an individual who suffered disconnection of the corpus callosum; he was found to have deficits of stereoptic depth perception in Sectors 1 and 3.

A third case, reported by the neurologist Norman Geschwind and depicted in Figure 4.6, also illustrates how a disconnection can contribute to visual deficits. The affected individual was rendered

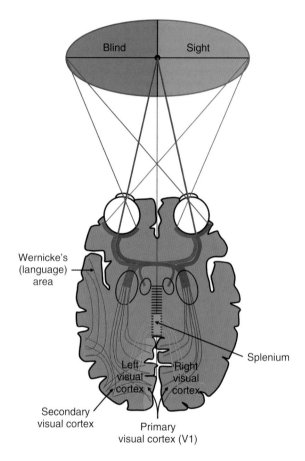

Figure 4.6. The damaged left primary visual cortex and the damaged splenium of the corpus callosum of a "word-blind" patient. Cortical damage is designated in pink. The patient's language functions were lateralized in the dominant, left hemisphere.

"word-blind"; that is, unable to visually recognize or read words. The insult to his brain was confined to two parts of the brain, the left area V1 and the splenium. Comprising the posterior (rearmost) part of the corpus callosum, the splenium is particularly important for communicating between the visual areas of the two cerebral hemispheres. It is also important to note that in all but a few people the left hemisphere is language dominant and thus critical for understanding speech and writing. But given the nature of this individual's brain damage, he would be unable to see a word ("SIGHT") located in the right visual field: The word will not be processed by his left brain, since his disabled left V_1 can no longer perform its usual task of processing the purely visual information specifying the word, for example, the shape of its letters. If, on the other hand, the word ("BLIND") is located in the left visual field, its visual structure will be processed by the individual's right V_1. However, because his splenium (the posterior part of the corpus callosum) is also damaged, his left and right cortical visual areas are disconnected. Since the visual information processed in the right visual cortex cannot be communicated to the left hemisphere, where word recognition occurs, the patient is again word blind. He might see *something* in the left visual field, but effectively this something is not a recognizable word.

These three cases exemplify disconnection syndromes caused by the severing of nerve fibers. The deficits can be very specific and can be explained by correspondingly specific disconnections. However, the case of word blindness reported by Geschwind additionally illustrates another neurological deficit that is oxymoronically referred to as *blindsight*. A phenomenon that has been studied most extensively in humans and in monkeys by psychologists Lawrence Weiskrantz, Alan Cowey, and their colleagues at Oxford University, blindsight is caused by a partial or total lesion of area(s) V_1 of the visual cortex. If the lesion is partial, for example, affecting a given locus in the left area V_1, it produces what is known as a *cortical scotoma* (blind area) in the affected region of the right visual field. If the left area V_1 is totally lesioned, the affected individual suffers from blindsight in the entire right visual field. Geschwind's patient suffered from a lesion of the left area V_1, and therefore would have blindsight in (a portion of) the right visual hemifield.

You may be puzzled about how a person who is blind can have sight. Here is a short answer. A person with blindsight will deny having any conscious awareness elicited by stimuli presented in the affected (part of the) visual field. Nonetheless, when prodded to guess about two alternative aspects of the stimulus, for example, its motion in one direction versus another, he or she will be correct nearly 100% of the time. To illustrate, imagine that Geschwind's word-blind patient is faced with the following two tasks. A word in fairly large, say 48-point, block letters is presented in the patient's affected right visual hemifield. After a short while, the word is displaced randomly either up or down without leaving the affected right field. Say that the word is "**WANT**." In one task, the patient is asked to report the identity of the word. He might be given two alternatives, the correct "WANT" and an incorrect one such as "OVER." When asked which of the two words was presented, he might initially protest by saying "What word are you talking about? I don't see one." Now if prodded to choose between "WANT" and "OVER," he is as likely to choose the latter as the former. So, over many trials he would be correct only about 50% of the time. In the second task, the patient must report, by pointing his arm up or down (even if he feels that he is only guessing), whether the word was displaced up or down. Here, despite denying that he sees a word at all, his response would be correct most of the time. In other words, the person's report of no conscious experience of the word is dissociated from correct performance in locating its displacement when what visual scientists call *forced-choice* paradigms are used.

When talking of consciousness, we step into controversial, if not murky, conceptual waters, stirred up by definitions that are not universally accepted. Blindsight is taken to be a deficit of *conscious* vision, that is to say, of (intact) vision accompanied by phenomenal awareness of what philosophers call *qualia*, which confer to each perceiving subject his or her privately experienced qualities of vision. For instance, for most of us the subjective sensation of red qualitatively differs from the sensation of blue and even more so from the subjective awareness of the shape or motion of an object. And for all I know, your subjective experience of red may be different from mine. For purposes of clarity in further discussions, I refer to *perception* as the registration of sensory stimuli in consciousness; these stimuli or percepts are qualia rich. Consequently, I no longer use terms like "subliminal perception" or "unconscious perception," although they enjoy currency in some scientific and scholarly circles and in popular culture. For cases of blindsight, I use the term *nonconscious vision*—that is, vision without visual perception. *Vision* is a much more inclusive term than *visual perception*. After all, a fly has vision, since it can detect and thus evade a looming object such as a flyswatter coming toward it. Nonetheless, I suspect that it has minimal, if any, subjective, qualialike vision, that is, it has no visual perception.

I use these definitions because they are implicit in much current thinking about the functions that human vision performs. For example, David Milner and Melvyn Goodale's distinction between vision-for-perception and vision-for-action is based in large part on what these researchers have garnered from case studies of, among other visual deficits, blindsight. The upshot of their research is that vision-for-perception and vision-for-action are (doubly) dissociable, implying that each relies in large part on separate neuroanatomical substrates. In some situations, speed of action is a premium. Hence, vision-for-action is fast; it relies on here-and-now "online" brain processing completed in a time regimen of a few tens to up to, say, 200 milliseconds. Vision-for-perception, on the other hand, is slower and depends on interactions with there-

and-then "off-line" processes such long-term memory, intentions, task strategies, deployments of attention, and so forth. Because of its relative speed, vision-for-action can proceed nonconsciously, that is, without phenomenal qualia-rich awareness.

To illustrate, let's consider the hypothetical case of a man walking down the sidewalk. A female friend across the street hails him and invites him to join her. He gladly agrees, but as he steps off the curb to cross the street, a speeding car approaches him. He quickly steps back, saving himself (and his friend) a lot of grief. I claim that his actions were guided by blindsight, that is, before he ever was consciously aware of the approaching car. Had he waited for his slower vision-for-perception system to kick in before he stepped back from the oncoming car, he would most probably be lying on the street in agonizing pain (or worse). You and I very likely also rely on a type of normal blindsight more often than we realize.

What does the experience of blindsight tell us about some of the functions that human nonconscious vision can perform? Petra Stoerig, who has collaborated with the Oxford group, summarizes many of the intact visual functions found in blindsight patients as follows: (1) They can determine the location of objects in the blind part of their visual field by, for instance, correctly pointing to them; (2) they can distinguish between a stimulus briefly flashed into their blind field and no stimulus; (3) they can determine the direction and the speed of a moving object (and may, in some cases, demonstrate a rudimentary, conscious perception of motion); (4) they can discriminate, albeit in rudimentary fashion, among the sizes, orientations, and wavelengths of stimuli; (5) associated with the first point, they can covertly move their attention to the location of a stimulus flashed in the blind field; and (6) they can respond appropriately to the emotional expressions in photographs of faces presented in their blind field. More recently, the Oxford researchers have shown that a blindsight patient (7) performed coarse stereoptic depth discriminations and (8) paradoxically reported conscious experiences of negative or complementary afterimages, for example, of a green square image, after removal of a red square that had been presented in the blind field, and that the patient did not consciously perceive. Despite their blindness to qualia-rich, phenomenal percepts in the affected part of their visual field, blindsight patients can nevertheless evince some rudimentary and nonconscious visual functions when the affected part is stimulated.

Still, resulting as it does from partial or total damage to cortical areas V1, blindsight has a global effect in the sense that it eliminates conscious vision of most any stimulus attribute. One can think of it as a disconnection syndrome (although it is much more than that, since area V1 performs sophisticated neural computations on the information arriving from subcortical levels). One thing that a lesion in or of V1 does is to disconnect *all but a few* of the corresponding neural signals originating in the lateral geniculate nucleus and to prevent them from being routed via area V1 to increasingly specialized higher cortical areas (e.g., V2, V3, V4, V5, etc.), whose neural activity depends (directly or indirectly) on the output of area V1. Recent research on monkeys and humans also has shown that, along with this increasing specialization, the neuronal responses at later levels in the visual cortical hierarchy (e.g., V4) are increasingly percept dependent: that is, they are correlated with the conscious perception of a visual object. In contrast, at lower levels (e.g., V1), predominantly stimulus-dependent responses occur, even when conscious registration of a stimulus fails to occur. These findings, combined with those on blindsight, demonstrate that neural activity in V1 is necessary but not sufficient for conscious perception. For sufficient (and necessary) activity, one would have to look to other, most likely higher, levels of processing in the brain. (On a broader scale, this sort of reasoning motivates recent neuroscientific research programs, for example, those outlined by Francis Crick and Christof Koch or by Gerald Edelman, who seek to find not only the neural correlates of consciousness but also its neural causes.)

THE BRAIN'S BANES II. CORTICAL COLOR BLINDNESS AND CORTICAL MOTION BLINDNESS

These higher visual cortical areas, whose neural activities become more strongly correlated with reports of conscious perception, are specialized to extract particular attributes of visual objects. In particular, it is now widely believed that areas V4, V8, and part of the inferotemporal (IT) cortex comprise at least a major potion of the cortical color processor, while area V5 (MT) is an essential part of the cortical motion processor. Another localized region in the visual brain processes animate objects such as faces, and still others process inanimate objects such as houses, tools, items of furniture, and so forth. Brain damage to any of these areas should manifest predictable types of visual deficits.

In the prior chapter, we noted that retinal color blindness can result when one or more of the cone types is missing from the retinal receptors of the eyes. In the absence of such a retinal deficit, a cortical color blindness, also known as *achromatopsia*, can result from bilateral damage to areas V4 and parts of the IT cortex comprising the cortical color center. An especially noteworthy case of achromatopsia has been studied separately by neurologists Oliver Sacks and Shemir Zeki; noteworthy—and especially tragic—because the achromatopsic patient, Mr. I., was a visual artist. The patient was understandably very depressed by the loss of his color vision. He no longer visited art galleries, an activity he had much enjoyed before the onset of his condition, and he described himself as if living in a

Figure 4.7. Left: Pictorial renditions of fruit and leaves by achromatopsic artist, Mr. I. Note the monochromatic nature of the objects. Right: Still-frame depiction of *Nude Descending Staircase, No. 2* by Marcel Duchamp.

(Reproduced with permission from Zeki, 1999.)

perpetual night, in which the visual world was cast in gloomy variations of leaden gray. His form vision appeared normal, however, as evidenced by his ability to render sketches such as those shown in Figure 4.7, left panel. And he would no doubt also be able to perceive the motion of objects through visual space.

In contrast, the female patient, L. M., described by vision scientist Josef Zihl and his collaborators, had bilateral damage to brain areas that included area V5 (MT) of the cortical motion processing system. Her perception of motion was severely impaired, particularly when she viewed rapidly moving objects. Rather than see an object move smoothly across her visual field, she perceived it in a sequence of "freeze frames," each consisting of a static object with no motion perceived between frames. The experience might be akin to that represented in Marcel Duchamp's painting *Nude Descending Staircase*, shown in

Figure 4.7, right panel. Such a deficit had a significant impact on L. M.'s ability to perform simple, everyday tasks. She had difficulty, for example, with pouring a drink in a glass because she could no longer perceive the rising level of a liquid in a container; and the pouring liquid itself appeared frozen, like an icicle. She also had trouble distinguishing people and objects as they moved toward or away from her. Because she could no longer perceive the motion of automobiles, her deficit was even more dramatically and dangerously apparent when she tried to negotiate a street crossing. Her ability to visually use her hands and fingers (e.g., to button a shirt) was impaired as well. This sort of motion blindness, or *akinetopsia*, may even interfere with certain social behaviors such as holding a conversation, since the perception of mouth and lip movements, on which "speech reading" depends, is impaired. One can readily imagine how such a deficit might also impair the ability to view, let alone enjoy, a sports event, opera, cinema, or a television show.

Image motion also is useful for the perception of form-from-motion. Consider, as depicted in Figure 4.8, a tree frog resting on a tree trunk. As long as it does not move, it is visually camouflaged by the texture and color of its skin mimicking those of the trunk. This is doubly advantageous, since, as long as the frog remains stationary, both predator and prey—as well as the amateur zoologist—are visually blind to its existence. Only when it moves does its natural camouflage become visible as a recognizable form. Many insects such as moths and butterflies also exploit this stealth feature, as do aquatic animals such as flounders and octopi by changing the color and texture of their skins to match the color and texture of the sea bottom on which they live. Would an entomologist or ichthyologist afflicted with cortical motion blindness have difficulty sighting a butterfly or a flounder, even when it moves?

Figure 4.8. An example of natural camouflage. Due to the color and texture of their skin, the tiny frogs sitting motionless on a tree trunk are all but invisible to predator or prey. However, if one of them were to move, it would become highly visible.
(Reproduced with permission from Bachmann et al., 2007.)

The types of blindness discussed in the present and the prior chapter are caused by some sort of genetic, congenital, or post-natally acquired defect of the visual system. Although such defects are unfortunate, they provide opportunities for clinicians and scientists to discover important properties of the human visual system. However, as we'll see in the next chapter, scientific discovery of these important properties can also be made by studying the visual system of entirely healthy individuals. Studies of this sort rely on using a variety of reliable, well-tested experimental techniques that noninvasively and temporarily suppress the visual perception of stimuli. As a result, an experimental observer can be transiently blinded to the entire stimulus or to some of its select features.

FIVE

EXPERIMENTAL
SLEIGHT-OF-HAND OR
Whoa! Where Did It Go and Where Did It Come From?

I n the last two centuries, scientists have achieved a status akin to that conferred on wizards and magicians in antiquity. They have mastered expert techniques—ranging from imaging subatomic particles, genetic splicing, and satellite communication to the detection of far-off galaxies—that would, so to speak, knock the ancients off their socks. And they still amaze, astound, and confound most contemporary nonexperts. Over the past 150 years, researchers in the field of visual cognition also have developed a variety of experimental laboratory techniques that are so amazing that they are deservedly referred to as *psychophysical magic*. As a method of study, psychophysics is associated most prominently with the 19th century German physicist and psychologist, Gustav Fechner. Briefly, the research methods he developed were directed toward discovering quantifiable relations between variations of the *physical* properties of stimuli, such as their luminance, acoustic energy, or chemical concentration, and variations of the corresponding *psychic* properties of these stimuli, such as their brightness, loudness or, say, saltiness—hence the term *psychophysics*. Eventually, this enterprise was generalized to include other techniques, some of which are clever experimental tricks, sleights-of-hand, that allow us to temporarily blind observers to certain stimuli without causing any damage to their visual system.

Over the past three decades, I have made use of several of these techniques in my own research on how the visual system processes information consciously and nonconsciously. These procedures—in conjunction with brain imaging methods such as the fMRI, the electroencephalogram (EEG), and the magnetoencephalogram (MEG), and with the study of neurologically impaired patients—have greatly contributed to our understanding of the neural correlates of conscious and nonconscious human vision. In this chapter, I will focus on several categories of these experimental tricks, among them techniques that produce sensory blinding, categorical blinding, attentional blinding, flip-flop blinding, and some other effects. You yourself can use many of these procedures and create their corresponding perceptual effects if you have access to, say, Microsoft^{TM} PowerPoint software and to a personal computer with sufficient speed and memory. You can also observe some of the phenomena I describe by referring to the websites listed after the suggested readings at the end of the chapter.

PSYCHOPHYSICAL VISUOSENSORY BLINDING

Since the middle to late 1800s, visual scientists have discovered several clever ways of psychophysically "dissecting" the visual system and of "skinning" conscious visual perceptions to reveal some of their underlying structures and processes. All these techniques result in a loss of perceptual awareness of a stimulus or a loss of what the philosopher Ned Block has called *phenomenal consciousness.* One of these techniques exploits the invention, in 1838, by the British scientist Charles Wheatstone of the stereoscope or stereopticon, a device for viewing stereo images that yields a perception of three-dimensional (3-D) depth. This device was an early version of the stereocameras and stereoscopic slide viewers that I sold in my youth while working in a drugstore in a small Illinois town. The cameras had two lenses horizontally separated by a few centimeters so that each lens would project a slightly different version of an image onto film. Once developed in slide format, the recorded images could be inserted into a stereoscopic slide viewer to yield a 3-D percept of the photographed scene.

Stereoptic depth perception similarly relies on the fact that the two eyes are horizontally separated by about six centimeters. Consequently, the projection of the visual world onto the two eyes results in binocular parallax or image disparities, commonly called binocular disparity. These disparities are used by the visual system to "compute" a 3-D depth representation of objects in stereoptic space. The images of the world projected to the two eyes match fairly well despite these small to moderate binocular disparities. But if the disparity between the retinal images is too large, for example, as in strabismic amblyopia (see Chapter 3), the binocular system cannot "fuse" them to produce unified 3-D percepts of objects. This results in what is called *diplopia*, the experience of double vision, or for some with strabismic amblyopia, in perceptual *suppression* of the input to one eye by the input of the other. Such suppression can be produced experimentally using the technique of binocular rivalry.

The upper panel of Figure 5.1 illustrates the normally fused 3-D object perception produced by moderate binocular disparities. Note the slightly different or disparate placing of images in the left and right displays. The lower panel shows the same display except that the two smaller circular images contain gratings with

Figure 5.1. Binocularly fusible (upper panel) and rivalrous (lower panel) pairs of stimuli. When fused perceptually, the upper patterns render vivid depth impressions; the lower two patterns compete as a whole or in a patchlike manner for entry into consciousness.

orthogonal line orientations. These two oriented gratings can produce a discrepancy of, or a rivalry with, input images to the two eyes that is so strong as to prevent formation of a single fused percept. If you have normal binocular vision, you can experience binocular stereoptic vision and rivalry by using the two vertical (central) black bars in the figure as alignment guides, and then gently crossing your eyes until the two black lines and thus the left and right displays perceptually fuse. Once they're firmly fused, direct your attention to the upper display and there see *one* large black-outlined circle in the background, with *one* large solid circular object and *one* smaller circular object hovering at increasing depth separations in front of it. These relative depth percepts of binocularly fused (single) objects result from the corresponding horizontal misalignments of the circular and hexagonal images in the left and right displays. Now, if you direct your attention to the lower part of the display, you should again see a smaller circular area containing the gratings that appear not as a single, binocularly fused plaid object. Typically, you'll notice that the left eye's horizontal grating or its patches and the right eye's vertical grating or its patches compete for entry into the conscious percept. In other words, this perceptual rivalry between the two eyes' inputs is characterized by patchwise or total dominance of one grating alternating with that of the other. What is important to note is that when one grating's patches dominate perception, the perception of the other grating's patches at the same locations is suppressed, that is, one is blind to their presence.

A second way to suppress visual perception is to use the *stabilized-image* technique or its easier variant, the *semi-stabilized-image* technique. Normally our eyes regularly move about in one way or another as we view the environment. They sequentially scan it for useful information or they might visually pursue a moving object such as a bird in flight. As a consequence, the images of stationary objects in the world are constantly shifting over the retinal receptor surface. These shifts are very important for maintaining visual perception of objects, for without them their perception would fade within a few seconds. This has been demonstrated numerous times by using sophisticated image stabilization techniques, which rely on the custom fabrication of a contact lens that, when firmly attached to the cornea, allows no slippage. In one version, a tiny projector mounted on the front of the lens projects an image on the retina, where the image remains stationary, that is, stabilized, regardless of eye movements. In another version, a tiny mirror is mounted on the contact lens, onto which an image is projected. This image is in turn reflected on a viewing screen located in front of the observer. As the observer moves his or her eyes, the image reflected on the screen moves in the same (angular) distance, assuring again that its projection onto the retina is stabilized. With either method, the perception of stimuli or their parts soon fades from vision. For instance, a stabilized letter, ⊢|, might fade entirely from view, then reappear fragmentarily, yielding something akin to ∟ or perhaps something more recognizable, such as the number ⊔. At any rate, the perception of the objects or its parts can be made to fade.

We can come close to experiencing this phenomenon by exploiting an effect first reported in the early 19th century by the Swiss physician and philosopher Ignaz Troxler. The Troxler fading effect, as it is known among vision researchers, can be produced by presenting a stimulus in the periphery of the visual field while trying to rigidly fixate a point located in the center of the field. Figure 5.2 shows a blurred gray disk above a small black dot. If you rigidly fixate on the dot, you should notice that the blurred gray disk will eventually fade from view, reappear, then fade again, and so on. Troxler fading can be accelerated and fortified by a technique known as *flash suppression*. For instance, if, while maintaining rigid fixation on the dot in Figure 5.3, you were to receive a flashing stimulus in spatial proximity of, or surrounding, the blurred disk for a duration of, say, 50 milliseconds, the disk will disappear from your view for somewhere between two to four seconds before it reappears. If this flashed presentation of the surrounding stimulus were

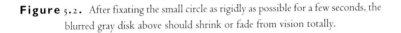

Figure 5.2. After fixating the small circle as rigidly as possible for a few seconds, the blurred gray disk above should shrink or fade from vision totally.

regularly repeated, you would experience what is known as *continuous flash suppression*. Here the perception of the peripheral disk is suppressed for the duration of the repeated flash presentations of the adjacent or surrounding stimulus.

Since continuous flash suppression cannot be illustrated here, a facsimile is depicted in Figure 5.3 showing the blurred disk shown in

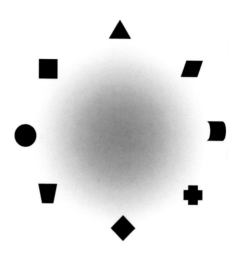

Figure 5.3. As in Figure 5.2., after fixating the small circle as rigidly as possible for a few seconds, the blurred gray disk above should shrink or fade from vision totally, but this time perhaps more completely or rapidly.

Figure 5.2 surrounded by high-contrast elements. Despite your trying to fixate the lower dot as rigidly as possible, you will still experience tiny residual eye movements. These movements will cause the images of all display elements—including, of course, the high-contrast surrounding stimuli—to shift across the retina, thus causing ever-changing surround stimulation. This simulates, however poorly, the repeated flashes and should render the dots less visible. In either single or continuous flash suppression, the observer is temporarily blind to the presence of the peripheral object.

A related phenomenon is known as *motion-induced blindness*. Here a stationary array of, say, three yellow dots located at the notional vertices of an equilateral triangle is placed within a larger array of, say, blue elements, which begin to move. When the motion commences, all three yellow dots initially are visible; however, after a few seconds, one, two, or all three yellow dots disappear from view, then reappear only to disappear again and so on in a fluctuating manner. Again the observer is temporarily rendered blind to a stimulus—here to a dot or a configuration of two or three dots.

An extreme version of the Troxler fading effect is what is known as *Ganzfeld fading* ("Ganzfeld" is a German word meaning whole field). Imagine that we divide a ping pong ball into two hemispheres, placing them snugly over our eyes, then illuminate the hemispheres with an external light source that is, say, red. The hemispheres, being translucent, will diffuse the red light before it enters the pupils of the eyes. Note that even if we move our eyes, we won't incur any image shifts over the retinal receptor surface since our visual field, a uniform red throughout (and thus containing no visual objects), is stabilized upon itself. As a result, we will initially perceive our entire visual field as a uniformly red space or "fog." However, after a few minutes, the redness will fade and be replaced, mostly patchwise but sometimes entirely, by a neutral gray, called *Eigengrau*, another German expression meaning "core gray" or "inherent gray." Effectively we become patchwise or totally blind to the redness in our visual field.

Although I occasionally have used some of these techniques in my own research on visual cognition, the psychophysical blinding technique that kept me most occupied over the past three decades is one that produces a phenomenon called *visual masking*. The idea behind visual masking is very simple. One stimulus called the *target* is flashed briefly into the eyes (e.g., for a duration of 20 milliseconds), and a second one called the mask, flashed equally briefly, is presented either simultaneously with the target or at variable time intervals before and after the target. When the mask precedes the target, the procedure is called *forward masking*; when the mask follows the target, the procedure is called *backward masking*. The task of the observer is to report on the visibility of the target (e.g., by discriminating and reporting its shape). The lower the visibility of the target, the stronger the masking effect. Not too surprisingly, the masking effect is strongest when the mask is presented simultaneously with (and thus spatially overlaps) the target and decreases progressively as the time interval increases between the onsets of the target and mask.

A form of backward masking that I have found particularly intriguing is called *metacontrast masking*. Here the target and the mask do not overlap spatially but rather appear adjacent to each other. The upper panel of Figure 5.4 shows two possible target–mask spatial configurations: a disk target (with an upper contour deletion) surrounded by a ring mask, and a vertical rectangular target between adjacent thinner vertical rectangles serving as the mask. The lower panel illustrates the masking effects of the first configuration. The reason for my (and some other visual scientists') intrigue with the results is that, contrary to the intuition that the masking effect should be strongest when the target and mask are presented simultaneously, the metacontrast masking effect is in fact strongest when the onset of the mask is delayed by 20–80 milliseconds after that of the target. In other words, at the optimal delays of 20–80 ms, the target is not seen at all—phenomenally, it is simply gone—as if the mask has a retroactive causal effect on the visibility of the target. At progressively longer delays, however, the target increasingly regains its visibility. Using the same stimuli, a similarly intriguing

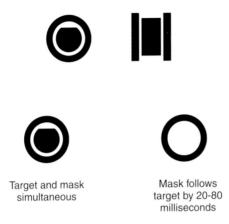

Target and mask
simultaneous

Mask follows
target by 20-80
milliseconds

Figure 5.4. Upper panel: Typical target and mask stimuli used in metacontrast masking. Bottom panel: Percepts resulting when a target (truncated disk) and a mask (surrounding ring) are presented simultaneously for a brief duration (left) and when mask follows the target by 20–80 milliseconds (right).

type of forward masking, called *paracontrast*, results when the onset of the ring precedes that of the target. The overall masking effect is a bit weaker than in metacontrast in that the target's visibility is not entirely suppressed. Yet here again the optimal suppression occurs not when the target and mask are presented simultaneously, but when the mask precedes the target by 10 ms or so.

TMS MASKING

A masking technique developed in the past decade or so relies on the application of transcranial magnetic stimulation (TMS). With this technique, a pulse issued by a magnetic coil passes through the cranium and transiently disrupts the brain's neural activity directly below the site of the pulse's application. In the study of vision, one can place the magnetic coil near the occipital pole of the cranium, the "bump" located at the middle of the back of the head. One can then flash a stimulus, for example, a letter of the alphabet, at or near the central foveal region of visual space in the retina. The stimulus is invisible during two time periods: when the pulse occurs either 10–30 milliseconds before or 80–140 milliseconds after the onset of the briefly flashed letter. For some observers, the TMS pulse merely disrupts the conscious registration of the stimulus; for others it additionally produces what is known as a *visual phosphene.*

You can experience a different version of a visual phosphene in the following way. Close your left eye and repeatedly apply slight pressure with the tip of your right index finger on the rightmost part of your upper right eyelid. While doing so, pay attention to the leftmost part of your visual field. If everything works properly, you should experience something like an oval-shaped grayish area as you apply pressure to the eyeball. This area defines a visual phosphene. Since the far right retina receives input from the far left visual field, it makes sense that the phosphene is "seen" in the far left visual field. By applying pressure to the eyeball, you temporarily not only produce a phosphene but also disrupt retinal neural activity at the pressure point, thus causing a temporary blindness at the location of phosphene.

Analogously, one can produce a TMS pulse-induced blindness in the visual field, sometimes accompanied by a phosphene, by interfering with neural activity in areas V1 and V2 of the visual cortex. I have participated in experiments that applied TMS pulses to the occipital pole of my cranium. The pulses induced an irregular oval-shaped visual phosphene just to the right of the central, foveal area of the visual field, as depicted in Figure 5.5. The phosphene effectively acted as a mask, temporarily blinding my sight at its location to stimuli presented about 100 milliseconds after the pulse was applied. The effects of visual masking by TMS pulses at 10–30 milliseconds before and 80–140 milliseconds after

Figure 5.5. Depiction of a small phosphene produced in the author's visual field just right of fixation by a TMS pulse applied near the occipital pole of his skull.

the pulse are thought to be very similar to the paracontrast and metacontrast masking effects described previously. However, despite rendering similar effects, the underlying mechanisms of TMS and visual masking are not identical.

PSYCHOPHYSICAL VISUOCATEGORICAL BLINDING

The various procedures just described exemplify *transient masking*, since both the target and mask stimuli are presented very briefly. However, there are procedures in which one can produce masking effects with stimuli that can be viewed for an indefinite period of time. Here phenomenal consciousness is preserved in the sense that an observer clearly sees something, but he or she does not have access, in other words, is blind, to its perceptual or cognitive category: The observer lacks what the philosopher Ned Block has called *access consciousness*.

These masking procedures take advantage of, among other phenomena, the *crowding effect*, illustrated in Figure 5.6. In the top panel, an isolated letter Y appears to the left of a central fixation cross. To its right the same letter Y appears surrounded by the four

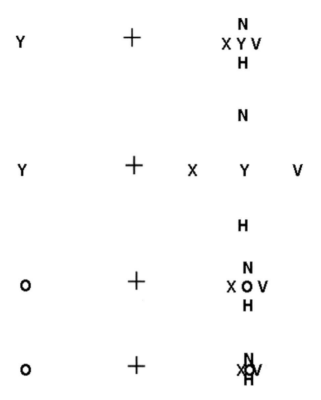

Figure 5.6. Examples of noncrowded stimuli to the left of fixation and the crowded stimuli to the right of fixation.

letters X, V, N, and H. Notice that the left-hand Y is seen clearly, whereas the right-hand Y can barely, if at all, be made out. Now fixate the cross in the next panel of Figure 5.6. Here in comparison to the upper panel, the surrounding letters do not "crowd" the right-hand Y as much, and correspondingly it can be seen much more clearly than in the upper panel. Now proceed to the next lower panel. In all respects it is identical to the upper panel, except that the letter Y has been replaced with the letter O. Notice that here the letter O is seen relatively clearly even within the crowded display. Why is the right-hand O in this panel clearly visible while the right-hand Y in the upper panel is not? The most likely reason is that the letter Y in the upper panel shares shape features (e.g., the vertical and oblique lines, and their vertices) with the letters surrounding it, whereas the letter O in the lower panel does not. Somehow the perception of crowding occurs when in surrounding letters the presence of features such as straight lines, their intersections, and their corners interferes with the visual processing of a surrounded letter such as Y that shares similar features, but not in the absence of such sharing of features between the rectilinear surrounding letters and the surrounded letter O. Only when the surrounding letters are very close to the letter O, as in the bottom panel of Figure 5.6, does some noticeable crowding occur. Recent brain imaging studies of crowding indicate that its effects are found as early as V2 of the visual cortex, where simple features detected by neurons in V1 begin to be combined to form higher-order conjunctive features that presumably are encoded in still later stages of processing, such as V4.

Crowding may also increase the difficulty of seeing a target object embedded in a larger display of nontarget, distractor items. Suppose an observer is given the task to detect as quickly as possible the presence of a short horizontal bar embedded within a display of vertical bars, as depicted in Figure 5.7. Experiments have shown that the target item is detected much more easily in displays of the type shown in the left panel than in displays of the type shown in the middle panel. Typically the time required to detect the left-panel target is short and does not change as the number of distractors increases. The relevant short horizontal bar effortlessly and simply "pops out" from among the vertical bars, since its detection can be made by discriminating a *single* simple "visual primitive," in this case either a size or an orientation

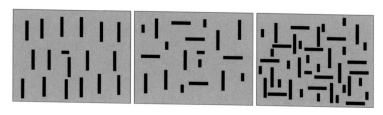

Figure 5.7. Examples of target stimuli that readily "pop out" perceptually (left panel) and that have to be detected in a more effortful manner (middle and right panels).

difference. On the other hand, the detection of the short horizontal bar in the middle panel is more difficult and effortful. In fact, the time required to detect a target in such displays increases as the number of distractors increases. Here one cannot discriminate the target on the basis of a single visual primitive such as orientation or size. Instead one must discriminate it from the distractors via a *conjunction of several* primitive features, in this case a conjunction of the orientation and the length of the bar. This requires a more piecemeal, careful, and attentive scanning of the display, thus also more time as the number of display distractors increases. Since overall spatial density or proximity of items increases as the number of distractor items in the display increases, one would expect crowding effects to become more powerful and thus to add to the difficulty of seeing or detecting the target item, as shown in the right panel of Figure 5.7.

Crowding does not entirely suppress the visibility of the surrounded stimulus. In all of the displays in Figures 5.6 and 5.7, one does see something, but despite registering that something in phenomenal awareness, one cannot clearly recognize or identify it. I believe these effects depend on another underlying limitation of vision, namely, the limited resolution of visual attention. In the science of visual cognition, a distinction is made between space-based attention and object- or feature-based attention. The former works like a "spotlight" or variable-power "lens" that can move about and focus on a particular location in visual space. The latter, in my opinion, works similarly, but in a more abstract "feature space." In either space, the task of the attentional focus is to enhance processing at the selected location (given by spatial coordinates in topographic visual space and by "feature coordinates" in feature space) and to suppress processing at neighboring locations. Hence, since the spatial resolution of the attentional system has been shown to be limited, stimuli very closely surrounding a target in visual space encroach into its space-based attentional focus and thus produce crowding effects in visual space (compare the upper and middle panels of Fig. 5.6). Simultaneously, stimuli having features very similar to those of the target encroach into its feature-based attentional focus and thus produce crowding effects in feature space (compare the upper and the next-to-lowest panels of Figure 5.6). This suggests that crowding is at least in part a failure of attentional processes. More examples of such attention-related failures follow.

VISUOATTENTIONAL BLINDING

One cannot at the same time attend to all of the objects in the visual world. Some objects do not register in visual awareness simply because they are not properly attended to or because attention is taken up by the processing of other objects. This is a pervasive phenomenon and can be demonstrated via a variety of experimental procedures.

A type of visuoattentional blindness that has caught the interest of many visual scientists in recent years is known as the *attentional blink*, or *AB* for short. The AB procedure, known as *rapid serial visual presentation*, uses a randomly ordered string of "distractor" items made up of, say, the numerals 1 through 9, in which are embedded two "target" items, say, two letters of the alphabet. All items are presented sequentially and rapidly—each for a duration of about 100 milliseconds (10 items per second)—at the same display location. The observer must identify the two target (letter) items in the sequence, Target 1 (presented first in the string of items) followed by Target 2. Of interest is the proportion of correct identifications of Target 2 contingent on (a) correct identification of Target 1 and (b) the number of distractor items (numerals) intervening between the two target presentations. It turns out that Target 2 is quite difficult to see when anywhere from one to three distractor items intervene after the correct identification of Target 1, that is, when the onsets of the two targets are separated by about 200 to 400 milliseconds. In contrast, if Target 2 immediately follows Target 1 or if, say, six distractor items intervene, Target 2 is seen more easily.

What is one to make of this failure to report Target 2 when one to three distractor items intervene? The gist of the explanation is that, at some level of perceptual processing, nearly all of the available, and limited, attentional resources are required to correctly identify Target 1 and thus are temporarily rendered unavailable to the processing of Target 2; hence, at some level, it is not seen. But if Target 2 appears immediately after Target 1, it often slips into Target 1's attentional "time window" and thus can be reported, as it can be when many distractors intervene, since the attentive processing of Target 1 has been completed by the time Target 2 is presented.

A related phenomenon is known as *repetition blindness*. Here a "target" item is shown twice in the sequence including other items, but its second, repeated presentation often is not seen. This could be due in part to the attentional blink; however, an additional contribution may arise from the fact that once an item is identified, its reoccurrence shortly thereafter is not a new or informative event, and hence does not register. Attention is a sparse and expensive resource and therefore must be deployed in an information-gathering way that is as "newsworthy" as possible; hence old news is no news. It is as though the cognitive system seems to be saying, "Been there, done that; let's move on." It may preliminarily process the repeated item, but then abort that process prior to completion, thus rendering the item inaccessible to perceptual report.

Another form of visuoattentional blindness is known as *load induced blindness*. Functionally it is akin to the tunnel vision found in *choroideremia*, one of the blindnesses of retinal origin discussed in Chapter 3. It is a functional form of blindness because, even in an intact visual system, if we increase the foveal perceptual load, for example, by introducing more stimuli that must be detected or discriminated in the foveal and near-foveal part of our visual field, we often fail to detect or discriminate stimuli falling in the peripheral parts of our visual field.

Related to this is yet another form of visuoattentional blindness known as *inattentional blindness* (see Chapter 4), a failure to notice something that is fully visible caused by attention being diverted from a designated target object by the presence of distractor objects in the visual field. Inattentional blindness can be quite dramatic, as demonstrated at a conference I attended in 2004. A film was shown of several young adults tossing a ball to each other, and the conference audience was asked to attend to the ball so as to count the number of times it was tossed from one person to another. While the ball tossing was going on, an interloper dressed up in a dark gorilla suit pranced through the scene, even turning to face the camera and thumping her chest before walking off the other side of the screen. The several hundred observers in the audience were then asked whether or not they noticed

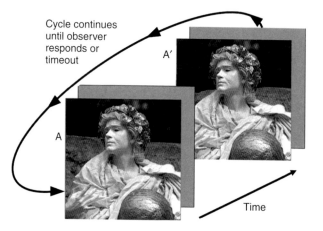

Cycle continues until observer responds or timeout

A′

A

Time

Figure 5.8. An example of a sequence of alternating stimuli, A and A′, used to demonstrate change blindness. The stimuli are not identical. In Stimulus A′ the stone wall in the background is lower relative to the one in Stimulus A. (Courtesy of Ronald A. Rensink.)

something unusual in the film, say, an interloping gorilla. I estimated that about 60 percent failed to see the gorilla. I did see it, but only because I had prior familiarity with this phenomenon and therefore knew what to look for. The observers who failed to see it presumably were naïve to the phenomenon and had allocated the major portion of their attentional resources to following the path of the ball and counting the number of times it was exchanged among the ball tossers. What little of their attentional resources remained was not sufficient to register the gorilla in their attentive vision.

In other demonstrations and studies of *change blindness*, an observer is presented a sequence of two alternating scenes, like those shown in Figure 5.8, where one scene is identical in all respects to the other except for what should be a rather obvious detail. Many observers are unable to see this differ-entiating detail until the alternating scenes are presented for up to a minute or more. Change blindness like inattentional blindness contributes not only to the repertoire of magical tricks used in the vision laboratory to render stimuli inaccessible to conscious report, but no doubt also to the bag of tricks of the stage magician and illusionist. As the example of the interloping gorilla described above illustrates, much of the action during a magic show serves mainly to distract attention from events that the magician does not want the audience to notice.

All of the laboratory techniques discussed so far in this chapter prevent visual stimuli from attaining either phenomenal consciousness or access consciousness. Despite these transiently induced blindnesses, some information about the visual stimuli, for example, information regarding their shape, wavelength, or emotional content, is nevertheless processed nonconsciously by the visual system, much like the residual and nonconscious visual information processed by blindsight patients. Indeed, although extensive comparisons have not been done, it would be fruitful to compare these experimentally induced transient blindnesses to each other and to blindsight and other trauma-induced durable blindnesses discussed in Chapter 4. For instance, some extant research already indicates that the transient blindnesses produced by binocular rivalry suppression and by metacontrast suppression occur at different levels of visual processing. Despite this difference, both types of transient visual blindness share features in common with the more durable blindsight. Further investigations of the relationships among these different types of blindness may go a long way toward understanding how vision works and how it fails to work.

FLIP-FLOP BLINDING

For decades visual scientists have used what are known as *multivalent stimuli* to understand how the brain organizes visual percepts. One particular type of a multivalent stimulus is called an *ambiguous figure*, which has two possible perceptual organizations that alternate in a flip-flop manner over time. Popular examples of ambiguous figures are the Necker cube and the rat/face figure, shown in the upper left and right panels of Figure 5.9, respectively. If you look, for instance, at the left panel, you will perceive a three-dimensional "cube" reversing in depth and spatial orientation. At one time, you'll see the lower left square as the front face of the cube while seeing the upper left square as the back of the cube. Soon there-after, you'll see the front–back percept of these two squares reverse along with the perceived orientation of the cube in visual space. In the former case, the cube appears tilted slightly downward in three-dimensional space; in the latter case, slightly upwards. Note that you *cannot see both* of the organizations of the cube at any one time. When you *see one*, you are *"blind" to the other*. Similarly for the right panel: Although at any moment you can see either a rat or else a (bald) human head with glasses mounted atop an aquiline nose, you cannot see both. While seeing one perceptual organization, you are blind to the other.

Perception psychologists have invented dozens of such ambig-uous displays, including nonstatic, motion displays in which the moving stimulus can be organized in one of several ways. One well-known example is the Ternus-Pikler display, depicted in the lower panel of Figure 5.9. Here three horizontally arrayed elements are displaced by one dot position from one frame to the next, then back to the original position and so on. If the interval between successive frames is very brief, one perceives the two spatially overlapping dots of each frame as stationary and the nonoverlapping dots as moving back and forth from one end of the display to the other as long as the

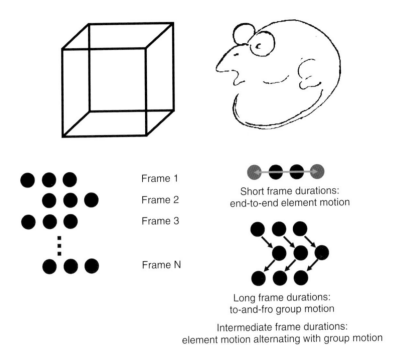

Figure 5.9. Upper panel: Two examples of perceptually ambiguous or multivalent figures, the Necker cube (left) and the rat/face (right). When one version of the stimulus is seen or perceptually present; the other is perceptually absent or unseen. Lower panel: The Ternus-Pikler display (left) and its associated percepts of end-to-end, element motion, or of group motion (right).

(Reproduced with permission from Bachmann et al., 2007.)

frames are alternated. At long interframe intervals, one perceives that the three dots move back and forth as a group. At intermediate interframe intervals, one can perceive both types of motion, but only one type at a time. For example, one might initially perceive the end elements moving back and forth but not see to-and-fro group motion. A bit later, one might see to-and-fro group motion but not to-and-fro element motion, and so on.

Current research is attempting to understand what mechanisms or processes control the dynamic alternations of perceptual organization that occur in these sorts of flip-flop displays. Moreover, these multivalent displays are important tools used by vision researchers to shed light on how the visual system functions when organizing its more mundane, typically univalent or unambiguous percepts—say, of the letters that form the words and phrases in this sentence that you are reading now.

COMING OUT OF THE BLIND AND A DOUBLE-TAKE

Occasionally, visual stimuli can "come in from the blind" by way of various visuosensory and visuocategorical routes. Recall the tree frog described in Chapter 4 (see Fig. 4.8): As long as this camouflaged organism remains stationary, it cannot be seen by predator or prey, but as soon as it moves, it becomes visually segregated from its background and is readily visible. However, there is a class of visual artifacts constructed by vision researchers that registers phenomenally in the visual field yet remains cognitively hidden either for some extended duration or more or less permanently.

One example is shown in Figure 5.10. What do you see in it? Many, if not most, people at first tend to see a meaningless array of gray patches on white background. If you are one of these people and if you persist diligently, you might eventually identify a meaningful pattern. A related case is shown in Figure 5.11. When read at a normal reading distance with eyes clearly focused on the text, it is again hard to see anything meaningful, except for a rendition of rather abstract, three-dimensional block elements. If now you squint your eyes or prop up your book on a table or desk and step back about 10 feet, you should be able to clearly make out the pattern. By stepping back, you effectively reduce the size of the

Figure 5.10. What do you see?

Figure 5.11. Is there a meaningful message in this display?

image projected on your retinae. This allows the image to fall within the foveal or perifoveal regions of the retina, allowing the entire array to be organized into a unitary gestalt. However, if you now go to the end of the chapter and look at Figures 5.14 and 5.15, you should be able to more readily see the meaningful patterns or messages embedded in Figures 5.10 and 5.11. Note that, in Figure 5.14, some of the white spaces between the gray elements in Figure 5.10 are filled in by black bloblike structures that appear to be in front of, and thus appear to occlude, an array of four meaningful versions of the same pattern. Oddly as this case

Figure 5.12. Perceptual recovery-by-components of an object. Left: Recovery is possible when line intersections (T- and Y-junctions) are not masked. Right: Recovery is not possible when the intersections are masked.

From Biederman, I. (1987). Recognition-by-components: A theory of human image understanding. *Psychological Review, 94*, 115–147. American Psychological Association. Reprinted with permission.

illustrates, allowing for a perceived partial occlusion can actually make things more readily recognizable. Similarly in Figure 5.15, which is a blurred or a much reduced version of Figure 5.11 and thus mimics what happens when you squint or step back from your book, a verbal message is readily recognizable. Reinspection of the upper right panel of Figure 3.2 indicates that a person with blurry vision due to corneal cataract might actually be able to identify the hidden message shown in Figure 5.11 better than a person with clear vision! We will return to this theme of size- and blur-dependent recognition of objects in Chapters 7 and 8.

A third example is a type of visuocategorical blindness produced by masking specific components of a depicted object. Figure 5.12 shows the same object masked in two different ways. On the left, the individual lines of the object are masked or broken up while the line intersections are left visible. From these components, the entire object, in this case a flashlight, can be visually recovered. On the right, the line intersections are rendered invisible while segments of the individual lines are left visible. Here, the same

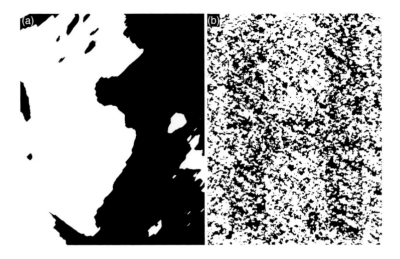

Figure 5.13. Two examples of difficult-to-recognize objects.

depicted object cannot be visually recovered, leaving us blind to its identity. These phenomena point out the importance of higher-order features, in this case vertices formed by line intersections, to object recognition.

A final type of visuocategorical blindness is exemplified in Figure 5.13, which depicts two objects. You may recognize one or both objects readily, or you may need some time to recognize them. Or like some of the students in my undergraduate perception course, you may not be able to recognize them at all, even after I identify what the objects are: on the left, the three-quarter profile of a young boy (hint: the profile is facing to the right with nose showing as the curved white blob on the right and the right eye to the left of and slightly above the nose, with shadow outline of his right cheek below the eye; on the right, the letter H embedded in a random-noise background. Now that you know their identity, it should be easier for you to visually identify the objects. But if you

Figure 5.14. Do you see now what you could not readily see in Figure 5.10? You should be able to see the letters q, e, and d in varying orientations; QED!

Figure 5.15. Do you now see the message that you could not readily see in Figure 5.11?

still cannot identify the objects, well. . . . What this demonstration reveals is that the visual identification of objects is to some extent driven by higher-level visual concepts (e.g., of what a face or an H looks like) in addition to purely low-level visual input (e.g., the specific stimuli defining these images). In other words, top-down influences from cognitively stored information about the world around us can influence how and what we see as much as the stimulus-driven bottom-up information can. In fact, top-down influences of stored information on visual perception can at times override the bottom-up information.

An experience I had many years ago made this phenomenon clear to me. While spending the Christmas holidays in Mexico City, where I had visited the former imperial residence of Maximilian and his wife Carlota, I bought the book *The Crown of Mexico: Maximilian and His Empress Carlota* by Joan Haslip in order to learn more about their history. Maximilian's older brother Karl was the Hapsburg crown prince and thus first in line to rule the Hapsburg empire. After reading many tens of pages in which the words "Maximilian" and "Karl" were used repeatedly and consistently to refer to the two respective Hapsburg princes, I came across the word "Maxl," the diminutive of "Maximilian," in a sentence. On first reading the sentence, I saw "Karl" rather than "Maxl." Since this out-of-place reference to "Karl" in the context of the developing story line made no sense, I reread the sentence to discover that what I initially saw was not what was printed. My mistake derived from the fact that my vision, relying partly on bottom-up data processing and partly on top-down hypothesis generation, had been dominated by the top-down hypothesis generation—and confirmation. Or to put it another way, my visuocognitive system had built up long-term expectations over the days that I read the book—as well as similar short-term expectations or hypotheses during any brief reading session—as to what names a long and short graphemic string should designate. For instance, given the two following sequences P#####A and P###########A, I bet you can tell me which most likely designates the city of Peoria and which the city of Philadelphia.

But what if you habitually referred to Philadelphia as "Philly"? It is possible that you might then mistakenly take the short graphemic string P#####A to designate the city of Philadelphia. On first reading, the unexpected word "Maxl" was a sufficiently close input match, both in string length and form features, to the word "Karl" that it confirmed the strong "Karl" hypothesis stored in my visual memory rather than the totally unexpected and, up to then, non-existent "Maxl" hypothesis. Perhaps you've had similar experiences when a particular context in effect generated hypotheses that sufficiently matched the sensory input so as to mistakenly confirm them in the resulting percepts.

Fortunately, in the vast majority of cases, our top-down con-ceptually driven expectations or hypotheses do correspond to incoming visual information, and consequently, our perceptions are veridical. Hence, errors of perception are the rare exception, although as such they can be quite informative about how our visuocognitive system operates. Indeed, the phenomena that underlie their occurrence also apply to other visual experiences, as we'll see in the following chapters that examine further how conceptual frameworks or cognitive contexts contribute to visual object or scene recognition.

PART II

BLINDNESS BORDERLANDS
Between the (Corpo)Real and the Metaphorical

*Our knowledge arises from two sources of the mind, of which the
first is [the ability] to receive representations (the receptivity of
impressions); the second, the ability to cognize an object via these
representations: (spontaneity of conception) . . . . Our nature is such
that intuition never can be other than sensorial, i.e., it [intuition]
comprises the manner in which we are affected by objects. In contrast,
the faculty of thinking the object of sensorial intuition is the
understanding. Neither of these distinctive faculties enjoys preference
over the other. Without the sensorial faculty no object would be given to
us, and without understanding no object would be thought.*
Thoughts without content are vacuous; intuitions
without concepts are blind. *For the mind it is therefore as
necessary to render its concepts sensorial (i.e., to attach to them the
object of intuition) as it is to render its intuitions intelligible (i.e., to
accommodate them within concepts). Both faculties or abilities,
moreover, cannot exchange their functions. The understanding is
incapable of perceiving; and the senses are incapable of thinking.*
Only from their union can
knowledge arise. *For that reason one ought not to confuse their
contribution . . . . [translation and emphases mine]*
IMMANUEL KANT, *THE CRITIQUE OF PURE REASON*, PART II.
TRANSCENDENTAL LOGIC

SIX

VISUAL AGNOSIAS AND NEGLECT

At the beginning of Part I, I quoted a statement from Aristotle's *On the Soul*, that all that is in our intellect is first in the senses. I take this to mean that not only our percepts but ultimately also all that our intellect grasps of the world around us with our concepts, even the most abstract ones, are based on or derived from concrete sensory experience. In the just preceding epigraph, Immanuel Kant, though less of an empiricist than Aristotle, also states that concepts without what he calls sensory intuitions and what I call perceptual contents are vacuous and, moreover, that percepts without concepts are blind. This is a terse summary of the relation of perception to cognition that will guide our discussion of visual agnosias—those deficits of visual cognition produced by damage to one or more levels of cortical visual processing. They are specific to the visual modality. For example, a woman with visual agnosia might not recognize that a given object in her visual field that, say, wags its tail, is a dog but recognizes it when it barks or brushes up against her. So the concept of a dog may be intact but be inaccessible via visually processed information. If you have read Oliver Sacks's book, *The Man Who Mistook His Wife for a Hat*, then you are familiar with visual agnosia. How can a man visually mistake his wife for a hat or not recognize what he sees? We'll try to explore this and similarly interesting issues in this chapter.

A CLASSIFICATION CHALLENGE

In my attempts to establish a clear conceptual footing regarding visual agnosia, I have very often felt that I am way out of my depths, treading in murky waters. It is a tricky topic, and I am by no means an expert on it. I have been reading about disturbances of vision and visual cognition for several years and generally have come to a fairly clear understanding of many of them. But although my reading of the published work on visual agnosias has enlightened and edified me, it also has confused me. I have found disagreements among various classifications of visual agnosias and, not unrelated, substantial overlap among the lists of their symptoms and causes. Some of the difficulty arises no doubt from the fact that these neurological deficits are due to uncontrolled damage to the brain, damage that is much messier and more extensive than that produced by a controlled and precise neurosurgical procedure. Consequently, the damage in any agnosia usually is not tightly localized but more or less diffuse, commonly producing a syndrome of several deficits. For instance, a patient with impaired recognition of faces may also have difficulty recognizing colors and inanimate objects such as cars or houses. In addition to such perceptual impairments, he or she may have impairments of semantic comprehension. This is actually to be expected, since the neurological insult that primarily or totally damaged the face-processing area of the brain may have collaterally damaged immediately adjacent areas such as those involved in color perception and object perception, as well as nerve fibers that connect a visual brain area with nonvisual areas processing aspects associated with a visual stimulus, such as its linguistic meaning. Such comorbidities are informative insofar as the area-specific functional organization of the visual cortex noted in Chapter 4 predicts them. But they pose a problem as to how to classify a patient by the deficits s/he manifests. Which of the symptoms is major or primary? Which minor or secondary? These diagnostic and taxonomical uncertainties yield some inconsistencies in specifying how symptoms map onto classifications. And classifications, though amply descriptive, often are not clearly relatable to causal factors. Moreover, although Kant distinguishes between a percept and a concept, he also knew that the act of visual cognition involved a union or comingling of percept and concept, two notions that I attempt to more clearly define below.

In theory and in practice, it therefore is hard to establish precisely if or to what extent, in the complex processes underlying visual cognition, visual perception and visual conception or understanding are separable. As is turns out, this (con)fusion of percept and concept adds to the difficulty in striving for clear distinctions among agnosias. From my point of view, all of these problematic issues call for a meeting of minds among neurologists, neuropsychologists, cognitive psychologists, and (neuro)philosophers as a very welcome first step toward arriving at terminological, taxonomical, and conceptual clarity with respect to visual agnosias. Fortunately some researchers already have contributed significantly toward this goal. In the meantime, we have quite a laundry list of terms—some broadly inclusive, others highly specific—to describe various types of visual agnosias: for example, *apperceptive agnosia, form agnosia, color agnosia, simultanagnosia, associative agnosia, integrativeagnosia, prosopagnosia, anosognosia, transformational agnosia, visual-spatial agnosia, object agnosia, category-specific agnosia,* and *topographic agnosia.* And no doubt this list is incomplete.

A DIFFERENT APPROACH

Whatever their formal classifications, complicated as they frequently are by taxonomic overlap and fuzzy boundaries, all visual agnosias share one common distinction: They are all impairments of *visual* cognition, of how we get to *know* the objects and events in our environment and their attributes through our visual sense. Visual perception, which I specifically define as *the registration in consciousness of visual sensory contents,* is only one part of visual cognition. As noted by Kant, the ability to connect the percept to a conceptual category is another component. Below, from the perspective of a researcher in visual cognition, I will attempt to give a clearer definition to our intuitive notions of percept and concept.

It is my opinion that the distinction between the Kantian percept and concept finds its analogue in the distinction between what has come to be known since the 1960s as iconic and posticonic levels of processing. One feature that distinguishes iconic from posticonic levels of processing in the act of visual cognition is that much more information registers at the iconic level than can be processed at the posticonic level. To try to get a sense of this, imagine that you and I are driving late in the evening through abandoned countryside during a thunderstorm. Suddenly a flash of lightning illuminates the scene all around us. For a brief period, you are aware (as I am also) that the entire visual field is filled with a rich array of varied contents. Now I ask you to tell me all that you saw. Like most people, you might answer "Well I actually saw a lot, but the visual impression was so brief that I can't recall exactly what I saw except for several trees to the left, some fence posts on

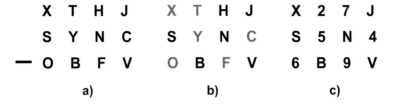

Figure 6.1. (a) A typical array of display items, consisting here of letters, presented briefly (for 50 milliseconds or less) to observers in experiments designed to investigate the properties of visual iconic representations of stimulus information. Over presentation trials, the letters and their positions in the display are varied. After a display is terminated, observers report either (1) as many of the items in the display as they can regardless of where in the display they are located or else (2) only as many of the items in a particular row as indicated by a visual marker as shown or an auditory cue whose onset is delayed at variable intervals after the brief display is terminated. (b) A typical array of display items in two different colors; in this case, black and red letters. (c) A typical array of display items two different conceptual categories, letters and numbers.

the right, and up ahead to the right a barn, and a piece of farm machinery that could have been a tractor."

To study the properties of such brief glimpses of the world in the laboratory, cognitive psychologists have used a technique illustrated above. Imagine that a visual display of Romanic letters such as those shown Figure 6.1a is briefly presented, say, for 50 milliseconds or less, to an observer. If we ask the observer to report as many of the letters as s/he can, we will find that, although 12 of them were presented, only about four or five are correctly reported, despite the fact that the observer reports also having briefly seen all 12 items. The cognitive psychologist George Sperling used the following clever technique to demonstrate that all 12 items were visually available. Very shortly after an array similar to that shown in Figure 6.1a is briefly displayed, an auditory stimulus (a high-, medium-, and low-frequency tone) or a visual stimulus (a bar marker as shown in Fig. 6.1a) is presented, indicating to the observer which of the three rows of letters to report. On any presentation, the to-be-reported row was randomly chosen by the experimenter, and therefore, the observer had no prior knowledge about which row was to be reported. Using this procedure over many presentations of different letter arrays, an observer could report (with few errors) all four of the items in any row, provided that the indicator was presented immediately or shortly after—say, within 50 milliseconds of—the termination of the letter array. At longer indicator delays, progressively fewer items could be reported from any row. What this means is that for a very brief period immediately after termination of the display, all of the 12 items were visible and thus potentially reportable. However, at a delay of, say, half a second to a second, only about four or five items were reportable when reports were summed across the three rows. By that time, the iconically encoded graphemic information had decayed. The interpretation of these results is that there is a purely visual, iconic level of processing, whose duration under these experimental conditions is relatively brief, followed by a later posticonic level of processing to which the information about some but not all of the items processed at the iconic level has been transferred and in which it has been encoded in a more permanent, posticonic form, for example, in terms of a verbal concept designated by the name of a specific letter. In other words, in these experimental situations there is a processing bottleneck between the brief iconic and the more abstract and longer lasting posticonic levels of processing that prevents more than about five items from the iconic level to be processed at those posticonic levels.

More telling—and this is important for our definitions of visual agnosias—are the following two properties of icons. First, in my own unpublished observations of this phenomenon I found that intrusion errors made by observers in reporting items from the briefly available display are determined by and large, if not totally, by visual, graphemic features rather than posticonic nonvisual ones. So, in the case of Figure 6.1a, an observer might misreport the F in row 3 as an E or a P, items that were not even in the display but, being visually similar to an F, "intruded" into it. Rarely if ever would they misreport it as a G or a U. On the other hand, suppose that I now allow an observer to inspect the same array for, say, 3 seconds, and then after waiting an additional 20 seconds I ask him to recall as many items in the display as he can. During this time, iconic information has entirely decayed, and the information about the array is encoded in a more permanent and abstract manner in short-term memory. Although now the intrusion errors may still be determined to some extent by visual, graphemic feature similarity, a large proportion of the intrusion errors turns out to be posticonic, in this case, verbal. Here, despite their visual dissimilarity, a D may be reported instead of T, or an A may be reported instead J because their names sound similar. Second, *nonvisual* and more abstract, posticonically encoded information is not as effective an indicator of what to report as is visual information. For instance, if the stimulus array, as shown in Figure 6.1b, composed of red and black letters is briefly presented and we instruct observers beforehand to report only the red letters, performance is relatively good in that they might report on the average, say, four or five of the six numbers correctly. However, if we now use a display composed of numbers and letters, as shown in Figure 6.1c, and instruct observers beforehand to report only the numbers, they might report only two or three of them. This implies that the information in the visual icon is encoded literally and concretely along purely visual dimensions such as color or shape and not more abstractly along some conceptual dimension or category that is alphabetic, numerical, lexical, or semantic. In other words, the iconic representation of information is purely visual as opposed to categorical or conceptual.

To summarize, the icon is a visually "raw," literal representation. Moreover, it is precategorical, in the sense that the information encoded in it contains no information concerning its semantic, verbal, or other more abstract cognitive or conceptual category. Such encoding of information characterizes posticonic levels of processing.

I do not want to give the impression that there is a simple linear bottom-up flow of information as described here. Since the 1960s and 1970s when the study of the visual icon was in vogue, much new knowledge has been gained into the processes underlying visual cognition, and many of these processes rely on what are known as within-level "horizontal" connections as well as between-level, "top-down," or "re-entrant" connections in which processes occurring at one level feed back to lower levels to affect processing there. We noted examples of such processing in the prior chapter. Moreover, there exist forms of visual representations and memory beyond the visible iconic level. Most of us can mentally transform abstract object representations stored in visual long-term memory by, for example, rotating, translating, stretching, or shrinking them. Such mental transformations may be particularly useful in architectural, artistic, or commercial design. However, these stored representations typically do not convert to visible contents in that they do not register as visible contents in visual consciousness except in dream states, in rare cases of eidetic imagery, or in rare abnormal or pathological cases of visual hallucinations. That said, I hope to have given the reader a better idea of what I mean by percepts, the conscious iconic registration of informative contents in the visual field, and concepts, the representation of objects that may be but are not necessarily tied to the visual modality, and therefore can be regarded as supramodal concepts abstracted from any of their sensorily specific registrations. After all, our concept of the letter H can be evoked via vision, audition, or in some cases even by touch. Similarly, our concept of dog can be evoked by sight of a dog, by its bark, or its feel, and sometimes even its odor.

For humans, therefore, the posticonic category may be one of many: for example, a modality-specific representation stored (invisibly) in visual short- or long-term memory, but additionally an abstract supramodal semantic category (meaning), an action-oriented affordance category (usefulness, purpose), and, as noted, a verbal category such as a name. These categories are not mutually exclusive. Knowing the symbol "W" via stored visual representation or via name also might be accompanied by knowing what it affords, namely, mentally rotating the image into a likeness of M or its use in spelling or writing or reading. Knowing the more complex symbol "WORD" by name also might be accompanied by knowing its meaning and its syntactic category—that it is a word, and more specifically, a noun, and so forth. This also holds for pictorial material and for that matter most any object found in the visual environment.

Since our everyday notions of percept and concept are fraught with much denotative and connotative baggage that renders them imprecise, for purposes of further discussion I will instead refer to the iconic and posticonic levels of visual processing as defined above. The distinction between iconic and posticonic levels of processing is functional. While some correspondences between anatomical and functional levels of processing already exist, much more work needs to be done by visual neuroscientists before we can get a clearer picture of such correspondences.

Given this (Kantian) visual information processing framework, I prefer to proceed with the discussion of visual agnosias by approaching them in three broad classifications: *iconic agnosias, posticonic agnosias,* and *disconnection agnosias.* The trained neurologist or neuropsychologist might protest this simple, tripartite classification, but in this chapter I am concerned more with rendering to the nonexpert reader a relatively clear, uncluttered account of functional deficits of cognition in visual agnosia than with adhering to the manifold criteria of diagnostic tradition. A chapter as short as the current one does not allow for conceptual carving along minor joints that reveal all of the fine details and nuances. For that reason, my classification scheme is based on the functional criteria defined above and not on anatomical ones. So, as we will see below, although an anatomical disconnection may readily translate into a functional one, it is not the case that a functional disconnection can as readily translate into an anatomical one.

To understand these three categories, let's consider the Arabic character, ق (Qaaf), and the Hebrew character, ה (Hei), as inputs to the visual cognition process. If we were to present a ق to an Arabic reader who is not suffering from any visual or neurological deficits, what would he see? He would of course see the ق symbol and be able to identify it as a Qaaf. But what if we covered this character with another stimulus (e.g., a black slip of paper)? Then the percept of ق, that is, its conscious registration as a visual icon, would obviously be nonexistent to this reader, and he would have no information with which to access the name category "Qaaf." This can be thought of, for example, as an analogue to blindsight. Or if we were to present him with a physically degraded character, for instance one that is partially masked, so that it would look something like the following: ق. Then he might have a degraded iconic representation of it that disallows integrating the components into a holistic percept, and he would again have little or no access to the percept's proper conceptual category. This can be thought of as being analogous to, for instance, a case of integrative agnosia. Both of these examples describe iconic representations that are either unavailable or degraded and partial to the perceiver, whose visual system therefore cannot use them to access their distinct conceptual verbal categories.

I can only relate iconic graphemes (the purely visual forms of letters or words) of the Romanic alphabet, for example, G A R D E N or G A R T E N, to individual letter, word, or semantic concepts (in English and German, respectively). I am barely familiar with Hebraic or Arabic script and therefore cannot recognize any aspect of it, not because I cannot see or consciously discriminate among the graphemic stuctures of these scripts but because I cannot relate these discriminable graphemes to known linguistic categories. I have no conceptual categories for the Hebrew or Arabic elements in my long-term memory, nor do I have the connections formed that relate the visual form of these elements to the lexical category even if it did exist. Functionally, but fortunately not neurologically, I suffer from something akin to a combination of disconnection and posticonic agnosias. These "things" register clearly in my visual consciousness, but merely as iconic representations rather than as otherwise meaningful or useful shapes. And therefore, I cannot recognize them in any more specific way than to claim that most likely they belong to some sort of script. At this point, I am *functionally* or *behaviorally* like an Israeli or a Jordanian patient who, afflicted with a combination of a disconnection and postperceptual agnosia, claims that *something* clearly exists in his phenomenal visual field but that he cannot find a precise concept of what is conveyed by that something. Not until I become very familiar with the scripts and form connections between the purely graphemically encoded information and more abstractly encoded conceptual categories can I overcome my functional agnosia and identify more specifically that "Oh yes, this (ה) is a Hei" or "Oh yes, this (ق) is a Qaaf." And still greater familiarity is required before I can visually recognize and identify words, phrases, and so forth, that use these characters.

Some Illustrations of Clearly Iconic and Disconnection Agnosias

For a real-life illustration of iconic and disconnection agnosias, let's revisit the case of the word-blind patient discussed in Chapter 4. Recall that in this patient both area V_1 of the left hemisphere and the splenium, the back part of the corpus callosum that connects the two cerebral hemispheres, are all but nonexistent. In effect, he is sighted in the left visual hemifield but suffers from blindsight in the right visual hemifield. If we were to present a word to his right (blindsight) visual field a few degrees from where he directs his gaze, he would form no iconic representation of the word (or at best a very degraded one), and although all other regions and connecting fibers outside of area V_1 are intact, he cannot access the appropriate lexical (word) category, simply because the iconic representation is nonexistent. He is an extreme case of iconic agnosia.

Now if we were to present a word to this patient's sighted, left visual hemifield, a few degrees to the left of where he directs his gaze, he might visually process the word in the intact right cerebral hemisphere and register it in visual consciousness. However, for lack of an intact splenium, the graphemic structure of the word, that is, its purely visual shape, cannot be relayed to the patient's left hemisphere, where the identity of the word corresponding to its graphemic structure could be accessed in long-term linguistic memory. That is to say, the word, seen in its *formal* aspects, cannot access, among other things, its specifically *lexical* or *semantic* aspect. Here we have an intact visual icon isolated or disconnected from its equally intact lexical or semantic categories (since the word would be recognized if it were spoken). Note that in this case the functional disconnection is due to, and translates from, the anatomical one.

Visual perception relies not only on the processes that allow for the proper registration of the features or parts of an object at the iconic level but also on processes at the iconic level that bind and integrate the features or parts into what are representations of the whole object. Although the icon as described above may resemble a frozen snapshot, it is actually an ongoing process initiated with the onset of a visual stimulus. For instance, a traffic sign, such as the "YIELD" sign, is triangular and has a given size and a yellow color. Its form consists of components such as three oriented edges, three vertices of different shape, and a specific color. After or as they are processed by the visual system, all of these different features or parts additionally must be bound in proper relation to each other in order to effect a holistic iconic representation of the sign. If our percept of an object is merely in terms of unbound parts or attributes, we, like some patients with visual agnosia, would most likely not have the iconic representation needed to access an intact conceptual category. So, iconic agnosias could result from a number of deficits, such as the improper or partial registration of an object's features or the improper or incomplete binding of the different parts into its holistic object representations.

Some Illustrations of Clearly Posticonic Agnosias

Are there real-life examples of posticonic agnosias, in other words, where a particular visual category is missing or deficient? The case of the woman I noted earlier, who could not access the conceptual category of *dog* despite seeing it wag its tail but could by hearing it bark, is one example. A person with *color agnosia* might be another. Unlike Mr. I., who as we saw in Chapter 4 cannot discriminate among colors because of cortical color blindness (achromatopsia), a patient with color agnosia can perceive, discriminate among, and match colors on the basis of hue but cannot name them. He therefore has severely deficient or entirely lacks name categories for the colors he perceives. I doubt that he has a general, modality-nonspecific concept of color. If he does, he would be like one of those rare individuals with synesthesia to whom, for example, the sight of the color red gives rise to a nonvisual sensation—say, an odor like that of garlic—while the color blue gives rise to an odor like that of roasted pork (I'll discuss synesthesia further in Chapter 7). Moreover, he would have to have established a strong association between specific odors and the nonvisual, odor-derived color categories.

A WIDER AND MORE NUANCED LOOK AT VISUAL AGNOSIAS

Using my tripartite classification scheme, I will now discuss specific types of visual agnosia, covering first those that in my opinion are predominantly iconic, then those that I believe to be predominantly posticonic (or categorical), those that I believe are instances of disconnection agnosia, and those that may be due to a mix of the other agnosias.

Iconic Agnosias

Mr. I. and L. M., the patients with, respectively, *achromatopsia* (cortical color blindness) and *akinetopsia* (cortical motion blindness) that I discussed in Chapter 4, present cases in which certain visual qualities do not register in their fields of consciousness. Like Mr. I., a patient with achromatopsia cannot recognize, name, or identify the color of an object *on the basis of a color experience*. His iconic representation of the object contains no color. He nevertheless may identify the color, but only indirectly by some sort of inferential process. For example, he might remember that the red, yellow, and green panels of a traffic light are arrayed from top to bottom. Hence, he can use the position of the brightest panel to infer the "color" of the traffic light. Similarly, like L. M., a patient with akinetopsia cannot directly, via perceived motion, identify the direction of motion of an object but might infer it from the changes of the perceived static positions of the object over time. In these cases, there is no color or no motion to identify directly, simply because the required qualities fail to register iconically in the visual field.

However, in iconic agnosias, failure to see an object or its attributes can result from factors other than damage to specific cortical areas processing object attributes such as color or motion. One such agnosia is *dorsal simultanagnosia*. This agnosia is produced by damage to areas in the dorsal stream of cortical visual processing (see Fig. 4.4) and most likely is a deficit of spatial attention. Both behavioral and neurophysiological studies indicate that visual attention in healthy observers can be deployed either to objects and their features (object- and feature-based attention) or in a manner analogous to a spotlight or a variable power lens to a spatial locus (space-based attention). What such mechanisms do is enhance processing of features within the object or within the spatial spotlight and suppress activity outside it. For such a spotlight to scan the visual scene, attention deployed to a currently attended object or spatial location must be disengaged and then moved to and engaged on another object or location. A failure to disengage from a currently attended object or location would not only result in the obvious failure to enhance the processing of a neighboring object or locations but might also result in its being suppressed (entirely or partly) from visual awareness, that is, from an iconic representation.

In dorsal simultanagnosia, the objects or attributes in a visual scene are seen and reported in a laborious piecemeal one-at-a-time manner, leading to great difficulty in comprehending the overall gist of, and the interrelations among the objects and attributes in, the scene. For example, while inspecting a kitchen scene, at a given moment the patient may report seeing a cookie jar on a counter but be visually unaware of all other contents of the scene. The next moment she may report seeing a boy who is standing next to a sink but be unaware of the sink and remaining contents of the scene, and so on. Moreover, she cannot scan the scene rapidly. It is as though her attention and gaze become stuck for an inordinately long duration on one object or part of the scene before proceeding to another. This may be due to the fact that damage to the parietal areas of the dorsal stream produces difficulties in disengaging from a currently attended object or location in the visual field. Additionally, the patient often *cannot localize* the object, *even when he sees it.* This might thus be an example also of *topographic* agnosia. The inability to know the location of an object seen in the visual field may seem odd, but it is not entirely surprising, since the dorsal stream comprises the cortical "where" pathway that processes the location of objects in visual space.

Another iconic agnosia is *form agnosia.* As shown in Figure 6.2, a patient with this condition fails to match a shape to its copy presented among several alternative shapes, and to render recognizable drawings of objects. This indicates that she has deficient iconic representations of the objects. When asked to indicate the match by marking it, she might choose those indicated by the dashed circles in Figure 6.2a. When asked to render a drawing of a shape, her results might look like those shown in Figure 6.2b. Neurologically intact humans can identify objects from many different perspectives, although the ability is usually easiest from a particular "canonical" perspective (see the Chapter 7, Fig. 7.3). In contrast, some patients with form agnosia might also exhibit a transformational deficit that impairs their ability to identify objects, such as a hammer, from unusual perspectives, as shown in Figure 6.2c; I'll have more to say about this phenomenon shortly, when I discuss it as a type of disconnection agnosia.

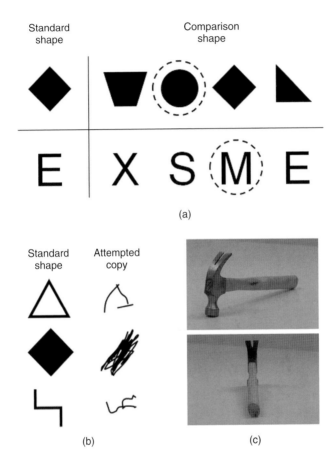

Figure 6.2. Form agnosia is characterized by difficulties in (a) matching a standard form to the correct comparison form shown among several alternatives, (b) drawing copies of shapes, and (c) identifying common objects shown from nonstandard viewpoints.

Integrative agnosia illustrates an additional type of iconic agnosia. A male patient, known as H. J. A., was phenomenally aware of elements in his visual field but could not perceptually integrate or group them into articulated and recognizable iconic representations

Figure 6.3. A drawing of London's St. Paul's Cathedral made by H. J. A., a patient with integrative agnosia.

(Reproduced with permission from Humphreys, 1999, Figure 3.1, p. 45, *Case studies in the neuropsychology of vision*. Hove, UK: Psychology Press.)

of whole objects or scenes. For example, while he eventually sketched, in a laborious and piecemeal manner lasting about 6 hours, a very good copy of an etching of London's St. Paul's Cathedral and its surroundings (see Fig. 6.3), he failed to identify the objects he had sketched. Other neurological patients, however, suffer from impaired recognition or identification of a visual event or object despite evidence that they have registered the event or object in consciousness.

Finally some cases of *prosopagnosia* may be iconic in nature. The recognition of faces can be based on holistic, configurational aspects of a face or on individual features of a face such as the eyes, mouth, or hairline. If, for instance, a patient cannot integrate the different features of the face into a holistic iconic representation, she may be suffering from a face-specific integrative deficit that impairs her ability to recognize faces. Or, if there are deficits of processing specific parts or features of the face, the patient may again not be able to recognize faces.

Posticonic Agnosias

On the other hand, other types of prosopagnosia, characterized by an inability to identify faces—including very familiar ones such as that of a spouse—can be posticonic. Here, abilities such as discriminating one face from another and matching two different views of the same face often are preserved. Notice that this is very different from cases of iconic form agnosia discussed above, in which, as illustrated in Figure 6.2a, the ability to match a standard shape to a comparison shape is severely impaired. Thus, in these cases of prosopagnosia, iconic representations of whole faces or their parts or features appear to be intact, but they cannot be used to access an appropriate cognitive category. For a normally sighted man, his concept of "my wife" is a composite of several familiar attributes: the sound of her voice, her scent, her touch or embrace, and of course her looks. Hence, the lack of any one of these modality-specific conceptual attributes would result in a deficient my-wife concept stored in long-term memory and thus disallow recognizing the wife via that modality, despite the image of the unrecognized face or its features registering iconically. Some cases of prosopagnosia can even result in an inability to recognize one's own image in a mirror. Moreover, prosopagnosia can be nuanced. Some patients *can* identify familiar faces but not their emotional expressions. And in other cases, the difficulty in recognizing human faces generalizes to animal faces. For instance, after the onset of prosopagnosia, a dairy farmer might not be able to identify his two favorite cows, Elsie and Betsy. In very severe cases of this condition, some perceptual deficits may also be present.

Most prosopagnosias are caused by a traumatic brain injury, but some are congenital, with genetic heritability indicated as a contributing factor. They, too, can present difficulties in recognizing faces of otherwise familiar persons. Brain imaging studies have shown that in persons with congenital prosopagnosia, the facial fusiform area in the cortical ventral pathway, believed to underlie face perception, appears to be intact. Presumably, therefore, their inability or difficulty with recognizing faces is due not to a deficit of iconic processing but instead is posticonic, due to absence of or an inability to access an appropriate cognitive category. However, further research needs to be done to test this conjecture.

Posticonic prosopagnosia can be dissociated from another posticonic type of agnosia, known as *object agnosia*, in which one cannot identify common objects such as tools, flowers, fruits, or items of clothes but can identify faces. A telling example of such a dissociation is the patient, C. K., who was able to identify the face in Arcimboldo's painting, *Vertumnus* (see Fig. 6.4) but was unable to identify any of the fruit, vegetable, and floral objects comprising its parts. Object agnosia can also be nuanced in that it can be category specific: A person might, for example, be able to visually identify items of food but not tools.

(Functional) Disconnection Agnosias

The impairment experienced by the word-blind patient described previously was a clear case of disconnection agnosia in which an anatomical disconnection in the patient's brain (the damaged splenium) readily translated into functional disconnections between percept and concept. This type of agnosia may also affect some patients with form agnosia, who, in addition to their iconic deficits manifested in failures to match shapes or in drawing recognizable objects of the sort displayed in Figure 6.2a and b, are

Figure 6.4. Giuseppe Arcimboldo's mannerist painting *Vertumnus (Emperor Rudolf II)*, 1590. Oil on wood, 70.5 × 57.5 cm.

Slott, Skokloster, Sweden; Photo credit: Erich Lessing / Art Resource, New York.

unable to maintain object constancy, that is, to recognize objects from different or unusual viewpoints. Thus, such patients additionally exhibit a transformational agnosia. Figure 6.2c shows two views of the same object, a hammer, with one view rotated relative to the other. Normal observers can, albeit with some effort, identify the view on the bottom, but a patient with transformational agnosia will have great difficulty in doing so. Presumably his or her visuocognitive system (a) cannot connect this iconic rendition of the foreshortened view of the hammer to its cognitive category and (b) has difficulty normalizing the rendition by "rotating" it, that is, *transforming* it, into a representation that can access the cognitive category. (Mental transformations, such as rotation, that serve to connect a percept to a cognitive category will be covered more extensively in the next chapter.)

In contrast to the iconic dorsal simultanagnosia discussed above, *ventral simultanagnosia* results from damage of predominantly the left ventral pathway of visual cortex. While patients with ventral simultanagnosia, unlike their dorsal counterparts, *can see*, that is, iconically register, multiple objects, they, like their counterparts, cannot recognize them. Ventral simultanagnosia has been characterized as a failure to *rapidly* process several items presented either simultaneously or in rapid succession. Time seems to be of the essence here. The "read-out" of information from iconic to posticonic levels of processing can be very rapid, to the tune of about 10 milliseconds per item. However, in order for such rapid connection between iconic and posticonic levels to be established, attention must not only be directed at a given object or spatial location, but also be deployed appropriately in time. Patients with ventral simultanagnosia appear to suffer from a deficit in deploying attention rapidly and, therefore, should—and do—have a difficulties with recognizing stimuli presented in rapid sequence akin to, but more severe than, the attentional blink experienced by normal observers in a rapid serial visual presentation task. A visual agnosia known as *pure alexia* (pure, because words can be readily recognized if heard) may be a specific variant or symptom of ventral simultanagnosia. Here words are not visually processed as a whole but seem to be analyzed and identified using a letter-by-letter strategy, which for a common six-letter word can, in severe cases of pure alexia, require upwards of 8 seconds to complete.

VISUAL AGNOSIAS AND THE VISUAL UNCONSCIOUS

In Chapter 5 we covered experimental evidence obtained from healthy observers that showed the existence of nonconsious visual processing. Similarly and perhaps not too surprisingly, most cases of visual agnosia, although failing to explicitly or consciously recognize or identify attributes, objects, and scenes, are able to implicitly or nonconsciously process them. The female patient, D. F., who has form agnosia, is a case in point. Studies of D. F. revealed clear evidence for a dissociation of her vision-for-perception and her vision-for-action systems. Although she, on the basis of her perceptual report, could not discriminate the variable orientation of an elongated slot, she was able to orient a handheld plaque so it could slide or "fit" into the slot. Also, faced with small rectangular objects of variable width (but constant area), she could not perceptually distinguish one from another. Nonetheless, when asked to pick up one of the objects, she was able to appropriately adjust her grasp aperture, that is, the gap between the tips of her thumb and her index finger, to the width of the object. This clearly indicates that nonconscious visual-information processing of the object's spatial attributes supported her visually guided actions. What the perceptual system denies, the action system asserts.

Although dissociations like this might be expected, consider the following. In Plato's *The Apology*, Socrates maintains that the beginning of wisdom or knowledge lies in recognizing one's lack of knowledge. Socrates does not deny his "agnosia." In contrast, a surprising aspect of some visual agnosias is the patients' lack of awareness, and often their downright denial, of the existence of a visual cognition deficit. The patients' unconscious can be tested for—and in that sense "knows"—this deficit, but they consciously fail to acknowledge that they do not know visually. This un-Socratic agnosia is known as *anosognosia*, a huge cognitive blind spot.

VISUAL NEGLECT

The agnosias just discussed result from either some partial or complete defect of iconic representation, conceptual representation, or connection between these two representations. Some failures to visually notice objects can additionally result from a defect of cognitive control processes such as the deployment of selective attention, without which visual objects or their attributes can fail to register in conscious awareness. Here, the parietal areas of the brain play a particularly important role. The parietal areas of the brain receive inputs from several of the sense modalities, including vision, the somatic and kinesthetic senses, and audition. Their multimodal nature generally is expressed in multimodal deficits when damage to these areas occurs. One result of this damage is a neurological disorder known as visual neglect, whose manifestations are particularly telling when the parietal damage occurs in the right cerebral hemisphere. Given that parietal damage in one side of the brain would have deficits in the contralateral behavioral field, the patient with damage to the right parietal areas of the brain would manifest a neglect, a lack of conscious awareness, of the objects in the left behavioral field. For instance, the patient will eat foods from the right side of the plate but neglect foods on the left side, or when looking at a face, he or she will report seeing its right but not its left side. Or the patient may shave only the left side of his face (see it as the right side in a mirror reflection) or have difficulties placing his left leg into the left pant leg when dressing. In addition, even when the patient does consciously perceive a stimulus to the affected, left side, its perception will be "extinguished" when an object presented in the contralateral, right visual field competes for, and wins, all or most of the attentional resources. This indicates that a major component of neglect is an attentional deficit. In terms of the psychophysically induced blindnesses discussed in the previous chapter, it is a severe form of inattentional blindness.

Some highly motivated patients can attain a nearly complete recovery from neglect if they pursue an active rehabilitation program. Figure 6.5 illustrates the recovery phases of an artist who suffered right parietal damage and therefore showed neglect of the left behavioral field. In the upper left panel of the figure is shown an outlined sketch of the patient's face before his neglect. The succeeding panels (b-e) depict a sequence of perceptual changes that occurred over many weeks and months following his brain injury. Note that in the depiction made during the initial stage of recovery (Panel b), the patient does not represent the right side of his own face, which falls on the left side of the depiction. Moreover, its depiction lacks color, suggesting the patient at this stage of recovery also may have suffered from (a temporary) achromatopsia. As the patient progresses through his recovery, he adds increasingly more form details to depict the right side of his face, as well as progressively more color, until finally he produces a full, if somewhat abstract, self-portrait. Note, however, that even here some evidence of neglect remains. Compared to the preneglect sketch, which locates the face slightly to the left of center, the "weight" or "mass" of the recovering facial portraits is

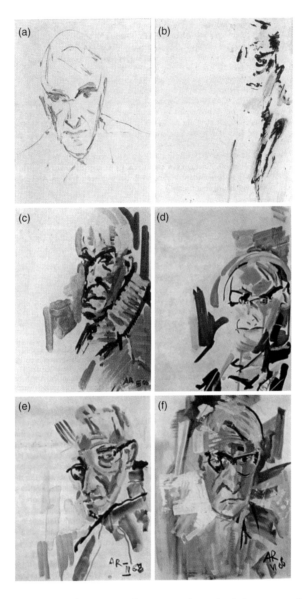

Figure 6.5. Self-portraits made over several months during recovery from hemispatial neglect of the artist Anton Räderscheidt.

Artists Rights Society, New York.

skewed in the opposite direction. This placement of the face's center of gravity into the nonneglected, right side of the portrait still was evident some 9 months after treatment began. We will revisit the topic of recovery from blindnesses in the next chapter.

This chapter has presented a compressed description of neurological damage resulting in deficits of visual cognition that cannot do justice to the complexity and range of diagnostic categories, or to the symptomatic subtleties of individual cases. Entire books, some of which are listed in the suggested readings below, are devoted to such extensive descriptions. What I have tried to do in this chapter is to highlight, especially for the nonexpert reader, four key components of intact visual cognitions that are lacking or compromised in patients suffering symptoms of visual agnosia or of neglect: *(1)* relatively high-fidelity and high-capacity iconic, concretely visual representations, *(2)* posticonic, abstract, and lower-capacity categorical or conceptual representations, *(3)* informational transfer and transformation connecting the former and the latter representations, and *(4)* an intact ability to deploy adequate attentional resources to the prior three components.

SEVEN

BLINDNESS AND THE MIND'S EYE

To sleep, perchance to dream [without the rub]...

WILLIAM SHAKESPEARE, *HAMLET*

*Thence forward was my vision mightier than our discourse, which
faileth at such sight.*

DANTE ALIGHIERI, *DIVINE COMEDY, PARADISO, CANTO XXXIII*

A picture is worth a thousand words.

COMMON PROVERB

In healthy individuals, hallucinations can result from extremes of
sleep or sensory deprivation, or from use of psychoactive drugs.
Recurring hallucinatory states also occur in some chronic afflictions such as schizophrenia. Whether induced by chronic
conditions or transient states, hallucinations are accompanied by
powerful and vivid sensory images. The same can usually be said of
dreams. Although some people report that their dreams are rarely if
ever visual and are dominated instead by auditory or kinesthetic
images, most people, including myself, have dreams that are sensorially rich and include the full panoply of sensory modalities and
contents. My dream colors on occasion are particularly vivid and
supersaturated hues, unlike any I have experienced in a waking
state. But one need not be in a full dream state to experience
dreamlike images. The delicious twilight states between

135

wakefulness and sleep, known when they occur late at night as *hypnopompic* and early in the morning as *hypnogogic*, also can generate vivid imagery. Less so recently than in the past, I have had hypnopompic states in which I experienced a movement of one of Beethoven's symphonies performed in full visual and auditory orchestration—without the cost of a $40 admission's fee to a performance of the Houston Symphony Orchestra. I have never experienced a hypnopompic symphony to completion. Usually I fell asleep way before the final flourish of the last movement, yet I never felt shortchanged.

As I tell the undergraduate students in my research methods course, dreams and dreamlike states can even serve to generate interesting research ideas and hypotheses. One of the most famous examples is that of August Kekulé, an organic chemist living in late 19th century Vienna. The story goes that he was attempting to discover the molecular structure of the organic compound, benzene. Kekulé first hypothesized that the atoms comprising the benzene molecule were arrayed along a roughly linear axis. He tested several versions of such a linear array in his lab, but to no avail. Frustrated and no doubt disappointed, he did what many of us do in these situations: he gave up—at least temporarily. Such temporizing can be very fruitful. Indeed, in due time, perhaps some early morning while dozing off in the street tram from his home to his lab, Kekulé had one of the archetypal dreams described in Carl Jung's *Dreams and Symbols*. As the story goes, Kekulé dreamed of a snake (in mythological terms, a manifestation of the reptilian *uroboros*), initially stretched out in a more or less *linear* fashion, curling around and biting its own tail, thus forming a *ringlike* structure. Startled by this dream image, Kekulé woke up with the revelation of a new, ringlike hypothetical structure of the benzene molecule, a structure that was confirmed experimentally in his lab.

Another, less well-known example of a dream that revealed a new research idea comes from the area of visual cognition. I arrived as a first-year graduate student in the psychology department of Stanford University in 1968, the year that cognitive psychologist Roger Shephard also joined the department. Several of my graduate student colleagues subsequently worked with Shephard, including Jackie Metzler who in 1971 copublished with him a very influential paper in the journal *Science* on a particular type of mental imagery transformation that has since been called *mental rotation*. The paper described how these researchers presented to their observers two two-dimensional depictions of three-dimensional (3-D) objects that, as shown in Figures 7.1a and 7.1b, could or could not be matched by rotating, for instance, the left image into the right one. After each presentation of such a pair of images, the observer pressed one of two designated response keys depending on whether the two images were of the same 3-D object or of different 3-D objects. What Shephard and Metzler found was that the time to arrive at a correct decision increased linearly with the depicted angular separation of the images. This result confirmed the reasonable hypothesis that, in order to perform their experimental task, the observers mentally rotated one image into the other. Success led to a "yes" response; failure, to a "no" response. This experiment was groundbreaking in its contribution to a reawakening—after decades of dreamless slumber in the coma of behaviorism—of the field of experimental cognitive psychology dealing with mental imagery. How did Roger Shephard come up with this creative research idea? As you've probably guessed, he had a dream whose contents included images of 3-D objects (akin to those that children often construct by conjoining Lego building blocks) that tumbled, that is, rotated, in space. Visual imagery and its "manipulation" in the mind's eye have been hot topics of research in cognitive psychology ever since.

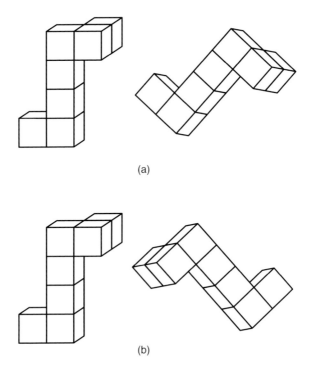

(a)

(b)

Figure 7.1. Examples of renditions of three-dimensional objects that (a) can and (b) cannot be transformed into each other by spatial rotations.

THE RELATION BETWEEN VISUAL PERCEPTION AND IMAGERY

In some sense, mental transformations like rotation, translation, expansion, shrinking, occluding/hiding, and so on can be thought of as real-time processes occurring analogically in an envisioned mental space. Some philosophers and experimental psychologists are, however, skeptical about the very existence of such depictive imagery. They regard the mental representations underlying this imagery as being more or less logically or propositionally descriptive of it, rather than analogically depictive of the actual experience of visual imagery. Over the past three decades, this debate has gone through several phases and is still ongoing. I doubt, despite the impressive range of experimental phenomena that Harvard psychologist Stephen Kosslyn and his colleagues have garnered in support of the depictive approach to visual imagery, that the debate will be over soon. As in other disciplines, the problems are as much interpretative as factual in nature. I suspect that both interpretations of visual imagery may result, at least in part, from interindividual variations of the ability to imaginatively visualize. During the latter half of the 19th century, the English scientist, Sir Francis Galton, noted that a wide range of imagery abilities existed among humans. In light of this variability, could it be that some individuals tend to represent mental contents propositionally/ logically, whereas others tend to represent them analogically/ depictively? And if a cognitive scientist happens to be one of the former individuals, could it be that he or she has difficulty imagining (i.e., mentally imaging) his or her mental contents in any way other than logically or propositionally? Similarly, a color-blind individual would find it difficult, if not impossible, to imagine colors at all but might expound propositionally and logically on them after having read a text on color vision. Whatever the case, I will assume in the following discussion that visual imagery is not merely epiphenomemal or illusory, that it can be something more or other than propositional, something depictively real and accessible to me, and presumably also to the reader, via each of our utterly private, solitary experiences.

Among those experiences is memory, without which we would live in the ever-present Now, without the ability for retrospection or prospection. Under such a regime, we would have no need and no way of generating internal conscious representations of either the known past (remembering) or the unknown but possible future (planning and anticipating). Our conscious images would be generated on the fly from the ever-changing flux of information impinging on our sensory systems. However, the human brain is not only a memory bank but also a memory machine. It not only stores but also produces contents of experience, by embellishing what is stored and conforming it to our biases and prejudices (thus confirming them). For that reason, many memories, rather than being high-fidelity reproductions of the past, can be highly flawed or missing in detail in their representations of past facts. Despite such flaws, memory is indispensable when it comes to generating mental imagery. For how else but through memory could our mind's eye generate an internal image of, say, a bowl of fruit and home in on a ripe peach, resting among black grapes, red pomegranates, green pears, and yellow apples, to see its skin tones ranging from a desaturated light green through yellow to a rich red glowing through a delicate fuzzy gauze, and to smell its—well—"peachy" aroma as our mind's arm and hand reaches it, grasps it, and draws it closer to our mind's nose?

Just as we use much of the same neural circuitry for storing and retrieving visual memories of objects and scenes as we do for perceiving, neuroscientists have found that the neurology supporting visual imagery engages many (but not all) of the same neural networks that are activated by stimulus-driven percepts. Consequently, many of the contents of our visual perception and visual imagery share common mental representations—or in some instances, share a common lack of both. The evidence for this derives from numerous brain-imaging studies of healthy human observers and from case studies of neurological patients. For instance, patients with achromatopsia, like the artist Mr. I., or patients with akinetopsia, like L. M., have lost the ability not only to see but often also to visually imagine the color or motion of objects. Some cases of visual agnosia that show impaired perception show associated deficits of visual imagery as well. These associated losses can be quite specific—limited, for example, to one or two of the following: faces, facial expressions, colors, spatial relations, object shapes, living entities, and integration of features into holistic representations.

The overlap of neural activation patterns used in perception and imagery is far from perfect. This is, of course, a beneficial feature: If there were perfect overlap, we would find it very difficult to distinguish current visual percept from retrospective visual memory or prospective visual possibility. Our ongoing experience would be a persisting confusion of experiences based on sensorially derived visual information in the present, visual information stored from the past, and visual objects or events imagined as future possibilities. Hence, there are by necessity some distinct differences in the neural circuitry used to generate each process. But as a result, and in some significant ways, visual perceptions do differ from visual images—at least those generated in a waking state. For instance, our mental images of faces are less distinct than their percepts because these images lack the detail found in the perceptual image. This could be due to the fact that our visual memory of faces is also less distinct than the percept.

If stored visual memories of faces (and other animate objects) and their associated mental images are less detailed than the high-resolution percepts, it may explain our relative difficulty with recognizing block portraits such as that shown of the author and "friend" in Figure 7.2b. In this figure's sequence, the blocking and blurring were done at a relatively coarse spatial scale. The result in the block panel is that we cannot see the "forest for the trees", that is, the global structure is noticeably masked by the local square tiles and their sharp edges. By correspondingly blurring this block image, we reduce the local detail (right panel), and a semblance of my face emerges but my friend's does not. The scales of the blocks and of the blurring were too coarse to render

Figure 7.2. The author and "friend." Panel (a): Original image; Panel (b): a blocked image; Panel(c): the blocked image blurred.

any recognizable details of his smaller visage. Of course, smaller blocks and less blur would have made his facial features more recognizable. Block portraits are sometimes used in television to conceal the identity of an individual. To remove some of the local detail in Figure 7.2b, squint your eyes. Are you now better able to identify the underlying global structures? If so, you might want to use this technique the next time such a block image appears on your local television newscast. Perhaps, to your surprise if not shock, you might recognize that the "masked bandit" is your neighbor living a few doors down from you. As noted in Chapter 5, a person with blurry vision due to corneal cataracts may be able to identify the bandit better than you having to squint.

In neurological cases, the distinction or dissociation between visual perception and visual imagery becomes apparent in a few ways. Some cases of visual agnosia can successfully recognize objects, say, an animal or a letter of the alphabet, but they cannot visually imagine them. In contrast, other cases of visual agnosia show deficits of visual object perception and recognition yet retain their ability to draw these objects from memory. Such double dissociations are taken by neurologists and neuropsychologists as *prima facie* evidence for distinct neural circuitries underlying visual perception and visual imagery.

Difficulties with the generation and "manipulation" of visual imagery are especially apparent in a particular type of agnosia. In Chapter 6, we noted that transformational agnosia results in the failure to recognize objects from unconventional viewpoints. But studies have shown that healthy subjects most easily recognize an object's shape when it is presented from the most typical viewpoint. Because it is most informative and highly conventional, this optimal viewpoint is the object's *canonical* representation. Figure 7.3 shows a number of photographic images of a stapler from more and less conventional viewpoints. One of these, located in the upper left panel, is most readily recognized presumably because it most closely matches to its stored canonical memory representation. The other portrayals are recognized with varying degrees of difficulty in direct relation to their deviation from the conventional or canonical view.

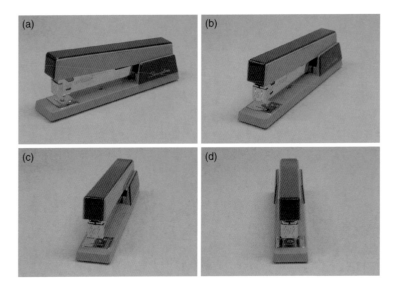

Figure 7.3. Photo images of a stapler taken from various viewpoints that become progressively less canonical from upper left to lower right.

Perhaps this difficulty arises because the less conventional portrayals do not activate the canonical memory representation as strongly as the more conventional portrayals. If this weak activation found in healthy individuals is exacerbated in those with transformational agnosia, it may lead to a correspondingly exacerbated difficulty in recognizing the unconventional views of objects. Patients with transformational agnosia may be lacking the perceptual tool, namely, normalization-by-rotation, necessary for matching a visual object to its stored representation. My hunch is that these patients, lacking this tool, would also correspondingly lack the ability to rotate objects in visual imagery. They would, in other words, have great difficulty with the Shephard-Metzler mental rotation task discussed previously.

THE BOONS AND BANES OF MENTAL IMAGERY

In my opinion, the ability to generate analog/depictive visual imagery is crucial in the practice of the visual and literary arts. A proficient visual artist can, for example, likely "see" objects or scenes with, or in, the mind's eye and could use such visual imagery to guide his renditions of it in some appropriate medium. Some of us might also be able to generate such imagery, but lack the skill to render them in any medium as art. Most of us, I must admit, simply do not have the mind's eye of a good artist. Without such internal vision, artistic expression would be severely limited. Consider a Michelangelo struck with an integrative agnosia and unable to imaginatively fill the blank ceiling of the Sistine Chapel with the depictions of canonical biblical themes, and the many saints, angels—the full cast of major and minor stars—each envisioned first here, then perhaps moved there, then erased and replaced by another and so on. Would he have been able to transformatively plan these scenes in his mind's eye so that they rendered a coherent story of creation, fall, and redemption? Could he have prepared the cartoons that would be pasted on the still wet, frescoed ceiling before applying his paints? I doubt that he could have accomplished any of these major and minor projects within the 4 years it took him to accomplish his goal—or ever, for that matter. Moreover, without visual dream imagery and its dynamic transformations, would an August Kekulé afflicted with visual agnosia have discovered the ringlike structure of the benzene molecule? Or would a Roger Shephard afflicted with akinetopsia have developed the experimental method for studying mental imagery transformations? Again, I doubt it.

If we were to extend this speculative pondering about Kekulé and Shephard to other scientists, we would, I believe, see that some other realms of sciences depend on such analog, depictive visual imagery as well. Without it, Albert Einstein would not have been able to construct his highly visual *Gedanken* experiments, in which he imaginatively viewed an observer's or object's motion near the speed of light, or an observer moving uniformly or accelerating relative to another uniformly moving or accelerating frame of reference. His special and general theories of relativity would likely have been impossible without such visual imagery capacities.

In my opinion, much of mathematics and physics also rely on such analog, depictive visual imagery. Take a look at the images shown in Figure 7.4. The left one, a photo depiction of a head of cauliflower, is an example of a natural fractal. Notice that the same basic structure replicates itself at ever smaller spatial scales. The right one is an artificial fractal that I constructed by replicating the same plant- or branchlike image at three spatial scales. Much more complicated images can be generated by computer to visually render what are known as Mandelbrot sets, named after the mathematician Benoit Mandelbrot, who worked out the mathematics of fractals. To do the mathematics, Mandelbrot relied on his gift of mentally transforming abstract algebraic formulae into vivid geometric images. Without such visuospatial imagery, he might not have ever discovered the geometry of fractals. Fractals are constructed by iterations of self-similarity occurring at progressively smaller scales. In the fairly simple fractal shown on the right in Figure 7.4, this can be seen by the same branchlike pattern repeating at ever smaller spatial scales.

Fractals have several interesting and counterintuitive properties. One is that their geometric dimensions can be given in fractions rather than integer values. Immanuel Kant some 200 years ago argued that integral-dimension space, in particular, three-dimensional Euclidean space, is the "natural," if not a priori, mode of organizing not only our visual perceptions but also our visual cognitions. Most of us think only of and with these

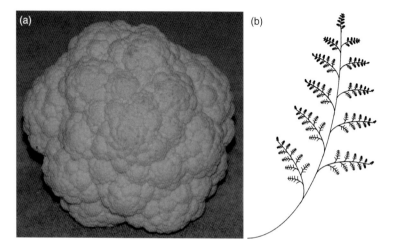

Figure 7.4. Naturally and artificially constructed fractal patterns. On the left, a head of cauliflower in which the more or less same geometric pattern replicates at ever smaller spatial scales. On the right, an image of an artificial plant or else leaf of a plant constructed by exactly replicating the same pattern at three spatial scales.

integral dimensions. For example, we think of any straight line segment as one-dimensional; a square as two-dimensional; and a cube as three-dimensional. We therefore are intuitively in the dark when it comes to, say, 1.68- or 2.54-dimensional geometric structures. For that reason, we tend to categorize structures such as the flat images shown in Figure 7.4 as two-dimensional rather than, say, 1.56-dimensional. Yet, despite our failure to intuit their fractal dimensions, mathematically such structures exist. They are exemplified in nature by crystal growth patterns, branching patterns of the arteries in our bodies or the veins in individual leaves (similar to the left image in Fig. 7.4), branching patterns of ferns and trees (similar to the right image in Fig. 7.4), the distribution of trees in a forest, the apparent irregularities of a coastline, a mountainscape, or clouds, just to name a few. Another reason that our visual cognitions can fail to register fractal images is the randomness or "noise" that nature imposes on the ideal geometry of fractals. Notice that in the photo image of the cauliflower head, a more-or-less same, rather than exactly same, pattern replicates at ever smaller spatial scales. Nature tends to always introduce varying degrees of randomness or noise into ideal fractal constructions. For that reason, much as we are unable to perceive block images when contour detail is present (see Fig. 7.2), we can remain "agnosic" to the regularities underlying naturally occurring fractal patterns when a lot of noisy details are superimposed. As we will see in the following chapter, a sensitive artist can hone his implicit (i.e., nonconscious) visual representation of nature's fractal structures, but only after a period of carefully trained observation.

Interestingly, the mathematical physicist Einstein received a Nobel prize not for his theory of general relativity, but for his prior research on quantum physics—specifically, on the photoelectric effect, or the ejection of electrons from a metallic surface when its atoms absorb quanta of light, known as a *photons*. Einstein was never keen on the subsequent developments of quantum mechanics, mainly because such mechanics are inherently nondeterministic. It is nigh impossible to grasp quantum mechanics through visual imagery, since its mathematical formalism is so abstract as to effectively remove it from any concrete perceptual experience. One of the leading quantum physicists, Werner Heisenberg, maintained that the essence of quantum mechanics lies in its mathematical formulae and is so far removed from our conventional percept-driven understanding as to be opaque to it. On the other hand, his friend and mentor, Niels Bohr, was more sanguine regarding the ability to visualize the atomic and subatomic world. He envisioned the atomic structure as a miniature solar system, with the nucleus as the sun and the electrons as the planets.

Recent work by Rice University physicists appears to confirm Bohr's visualizable model.

This difference between visualizable and abstract science is akin, in my experience, to that between geometry and abstract algebra. As an undergraduate, I studied mathematics as my major subject. Somehow, in my course on algebra, I often had to grope through the formalisms of algebraic structures, my "blindness" accompanied by a lack of surety, whereas in a geometry course, imagery was an often-used visual aid as I maneuvered through geometric spaces. While working such algebraic concepts, I felt that I was walking in the dark and seeing only in front of me what falls into the beam of a flashlight, or that I was relying on hearsay as to the direction I was taking; I would come to an understanding of the bigger picture only after arriving at the final formal step to the solution of an abstract problem. In contrast, while working out a geometric problem—at least up to three dimensions—I felt accompanied by plain-to-see, steady guides, each intuitively reassuring me that I'd see an wider view opening at the end of each segment of the proof's maze. Intuitive versus formalistic, analog/depictive versus propositional/descriptive: these seem to be the antipodal styles of making thoughts—mental images ranging over the concrete and the abstract—possible.

Are there downsides to the visually depictive imagery provided by the mind's eye? Indeed there are. Consider two types of visual experiences: one arising from activation of eidetic memory, more commonly known as photographic memory; the other from synesthesia. Eidetikers presumably can evoke an exact internal image of a previously viewed visual scene and inspect it with the mind's eye. Such memory is often considered a boon. After all, what student would not like to peruse a chemical formulary or an epic poem the night before a test and the next day read verbatim from their eidetically reconstructed images the answers to their exam questions? According to research, many of us were eideti-kers, to a greater or lesser extent, in our childhoods but lost this ability as we grew older. Some rare adults, however, have retained the gift. I became acquainted with one such person during my graduate studies at Stanford. She had studied German literature, which pleased me both because my native language is German and because I am, to this day, a "recovering humanities major." I happened to be reading Schiller's *Gedichte und Balladen*, and asked her to pick one of its pages at random, inspect it for a brief while, and then, a week or so later, recite its contents, down to exact punctuation. She declined, but reassured me that this was some-thing she could easily do.

Some years later in Houston, I became acquainted with another such individual, a successful young architect. On some occasions he could deliberately recall drawings, sketches, or plans as easily as a present-day architect or design artist can bring up a CAD image on a computer. However, the appearance of his eidetic imagery was not always at his behest. On rare occasions, when he was inspecting or preparing an architectural plan, unrelated eidetic images would spontaneously and involuntarily come into view and, by acting as a visual mask, interfere with his ongoing work. Sometimes this intrusive imagery was so uncontrollably persistent as to force him to postpone his architectural work until the eidetic image eventually faded from view.

Synesthesia, the ability to have experiences in one sensory modality induced by stimulation of another, also can be a boon or bane. Some synethetes' tactile sensations may be accompanied by experiences of color or scent. Other synesthetes may experi-ence a color when they hear or see a letter or a number, or experience a taste or color when they hear a musical note. Still others may experience distinct colors associated with particular food items.

Neuroscientists such as Vilayanur (V. S.) Ramachandran use synesthesia as a way of understanding the functional architecture of the human brain. At the current level of understanding, we can say that in some people certain parts of the brain may be cross-wired with other parts, particularly if they are anatomically close to each other, although the reason for, and details of, the cross-wiring are not known with certainty. For instance, the cortical color center in humans may be cross-wired with the nearby part of the brain that allows us to visually process numbers. Such cross-wiring may allow us to see some objects better, as evident in some synesthetes. For example, V. S. Ramachandran and Edward Hubble have studied number synesthetes who experience, say, the number 2 in red, but not the number 5. If shown the left-hand panel of Figure 7.5, in which a triangle-shaped array of black 2s is embedded within a random array of black 5s, these synthesthetes might see it as shown in the right-hand panel, with the 2s colored red. Normal observers would only see the all-black numbers in the left-hand panel and would have appreciable difficulty seeing the triangular array of black 2s in it because of the effects of visual crowding and because the triangular array of these 2s can only be inferred from their piecemeal attentive processing (see Chapter 5).

If these results are valid, then one should be able to reverse the effects of the synesthetic experience to produce a relative blinding. For instance, if we color red the 5s depicted in the left-hand panel of Figure 7.5 and leave the 2s black, we would expect the black triangular array of 2s to pop out perceptually for the normal perceiver but to be much more difficult for the number synesthete to see because all the numbers in the panel would then appear red. As with many other things, the benefits or costs of an unusual ability depend on context. Moreover, like the eidetic images of eidetikers, the experiences of synesthetic colors by synesthetes do

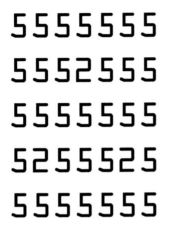 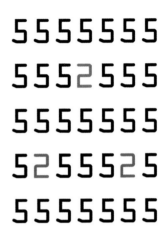

Figure 7.5. The left and the right arrays of numerals contain a triangle-shaped array of three 2s among 5s. The left array depicts what a normal observer sees; the right array, what a synesthete might see.

not occur at their beck and call but rather leave them at the mercy of the inducing stimulus. Despite these actual or possible inconveniences, synesthesia, as noted by V. S. Ramachandran, may be a boon to artists and poets, amplifying their ability to express themselves metaphorically in language and imaginatively in art.

I have already noted the internally generated, hallucinatory experiences of some patients with schizophrenia. These can be as vivid and as convincing as experiences based on perception of objects and events in the external world. And the images that hallucinations can generate are generally a disturbing bane to those who suffer them. Healthy individuals usually know when they experience a hallucination, say, due to sleep deprivation. That is to say, they have good metacognitive skills, which allow them to reflect or think about their percept- or concept-driven cognitions in a detached manner. Many individuals with schizophrenia tend to be deficient in this skill. In the movie script of *A Beautiful Mind*, a modified adaptation of Sylvia Nasar's same-titled book, the math-whiz protagonist, John Nash, has hallucinations of a young man and a little girl. Only when he notes, after years of experiencing these hallucinations, that the young man and little girl do not mature or age as would be reasonably expected, does he come to realize that he had been blind to the reality of their nonexistence. As a Nobel-laureate genius and thus a highly rational schizophrenic, the cinematic John Nash was able to logically deduce their nonexistence despite their continuing hallucinatory appearances.

A FURTHER BOON OF VISUAL IMAGERY

I would like to make some remarks about recovery from various types of blindness and the role of visual imagery in such recovery. In Chapter 3, I mentioned Richard Gregory and Jean Wallace's investigation of an individual who underwent surgery for corneal opacity. By all accounts, his recovery from partial blindness did not go too well. Functional recovery from neurologically caused visual deficits can be more successful but often requires much time and effort. An example, noted in Chapter 6, was the recovery of the right-parietal-neglect patient. Unfortunately for some neurological cases of blindness, no amount of rehabilitation or effort will totally undo the loss of visual ability. The achromatopsic patient Mr. I. will most likely never recover his color vision, nor will the female patient L. M., who suffered from akinetopsia, recover her motion perception. Blindsight patients may regain some vision because the size of the scotoma (blind area) in their affected visual field may shrink to some extent as recovery progresses; however, a residual scotoma usually persists. That they can still discriminate wavelengths has prompted some philosophers to wonder whether such patients, if trained repeatedly and sufficiently in making wavelength discriminations, would eventually recover conscious color vision. Although I am open to pleasant surprises, I consider this to be a most unlikely outcome. I believe that a behaviorist/functionalist view of consciousness would founder here. There are biological limits to the human spirit that training and remediation will not overcome.

Josef Zihl's monograph, *Rehabilitation of Visual Deficits After Brain Injury*, covers evidence and cases of spontaneous recoveries and of restitutions of some functions. However, the latter usually occur only with laborious and intensive rehabilitative training. And the extent of recovery depends on when the initial damage occurred. For example, due to the high degree of plasticity of the developing brain shortly after birth, functional recovery after neurological damage in infancy is much more likely than recovery after neurological damage in adulthood. In an adult, much of the mind's "software," including its color software, runs on specialized brain hardware such as V_4 and on the wavelength- and color-specific processing hardware in cortical areas V_1/V_2. If those areas are damaged, restoration of color vision will be limited and noticeable deficits will nonetheless persist. However, even if no restoration is possible, one can deal with the loss of function through compensatory behaviors that in one way or another circumvent the limits and make use of whatever residual vision one still has. Imagine the following. A blindsight patient suffers from a large scotoma that covers most but not all of her visual field. By moving her eyes into position so that the image of an object falls on those parts of the two eyes' retinae that project to the spared regions in V_1, she could consciously experience most objects in her highly limited visual field. Her "recovery" of (conscious) vision could rely on acquiring (i.e., learning) such a compensatory strategy.

Now to the other topic of this section, the role of visual imagery in "recovery" from blindness. I have again placed the word *recovery* in quotes, because it, like the hypothetical example of recovery just given, relies on a compensatory process. Of course, if you suffer from a brain injury, such as visual agnosia or achromatopsia, that causes not only perceptual but also imagery deficits, recovery based on exploiting visual imagery would be all but impossible. But for those whose visual brain areas are for the most part anatomically and functionally intact and whose blindness is produced by an "upstream" trauma, for example, damage done to the retinae of the lateral geniculate nuclei, then the use of visual imagery can be extremely helpful.

In the 1980s, a blind man in his mid-thirties enrolled in my undergraduate course on perception. About a decade earlier, he had been in a chemical accident that resulted in his total retinal blindness. Although he could no longer see objects or scenes in the external world, he had dreams with visual content, and he could generate visual imagery at will. Moreover, he would often have spontaneous visual sensations accompanying some auditory or kinesthetic ones. For instance, the sound of a passing car would generate a visual impression akin to a shadow moving through his blind field. His capacity for visual imagery also served him at home, where he visualized its spatial layout, thereby facilitating his orientation to and mobility throughout various parts of his house.

A dramatic account of such a visual image-based recovery was delivered by psychologist Zoltan Torey at the 2004 conference, *Toward a Science of Consciousness*, held in Tucson, Arizona. Also retinally blinded in adulthood as a result of work-related accident, Torey honed his previously underutilized ability to visually image his environment to a degree of perfection that it eventually allowed him to create within his mind a highly faithful visual representation of his home and its immediate surroundings. By his account, he could clearly and consciously experience his immediate world in a visual modality. With brief flourishes of humor, he recounted an episode when his neighbors—who were aware of his blindness—expressed surprise at watching him attach rain gutters along the entire roof of his house. Piece by piece he hammered and nailed the gutters to the eaves of the roof, joined gutter segments correctly, advanced his ladder and tools, and performed all of the other tasks of an expert sighted roofer. Truly amazing feats! Of course, when in unfamiliar environs, such as the conference setting in Tucson, he relied heavily on the guidance of a companion. However, given sufficient time, his acquired visual imaging skills would no doubt have allowed him eventually to consciously image the setting, thus providing him with its "virtual" visual reality.

Torey's acquired ability to *create* highly nuanced, qualia-rich visual images is indeed an amazing feat, and his life as a whole has been an amazing work of visual and literary art. His published accounts of his struggle to emerge from darkness into a surrogate form of conscious vision make for excellent reading because they are not only an interesting case study but also wonderful literary works by a man of true vision. Much like the deepened and broadened imaginative prowess expressed in the collection of poetry, *In Praise of Darkness*, by the Argentinian poet Jorge Luis Borges when his sight was lost to advancing glaucoma, Zoltan Torey's accomplishments demonstrate how sometimes the destructive reality of blindness can be transformed by the human spirit through creative metaphors.

PART III

BLINDNESS METAPHORICAL

Vision in its literal sense contributes to knowledge or understanding, but that contribution is less than total. There are many ways of knowing, from the sensorially immediate and concrete to the conceptually remote and abstract. Thus, the words "eye," "seeing," "sight," "light," "illumination," "darkness," and "blindness" and their many cognates are, beyond their literal meanings, figures of speech, synecdoches that act as *pars pro toto*. Their metaphoric use in many scholarly and literary endeavors has a very long history, going back to antiquity. They also appear in abundance in our own time, for example, in two parabolic works, *Seeing* and *Blindness*, by the Portuguese novelist and poet José Saramago. More generally, we all talk metaphorically of seeing as a way of discovering; of illumination as understanding attained; of view and perspective as conceptual stances taken toward an object; of a perceptive or perspicacious remark, a myopic or blinkered understanding, or a grand and lofty vision as a capacious and comprehensive understanding of a field of knowledge or action. Moreover, our language is full of metaphors that are spatial in origin. And since, for most of us, the dominant spatial sense is vision, these metaphors are visual in origin as well. Hence we talk of insight, oversight, hindsight, and foresight. And as antitheses of "sight" and "light," "blindness" and "darkness" are apt metaphors for the failure to grasp an idea or concept, for a state of ignorance or misconception. How often, when unable to convince someone of a point that is clear to us, do we plead "Can't you see that?", "Are you blind?", or "Open your eyes to the facts!"? At other times, when someone tries to hoodwink or mislead us, we say "I can see through their ruse." And we talk of the seer and visionary who have prophetic foresight and clairvoyance. The list of usages of sight and light and of blindness and darkness as metaphors is seemingly endless.

EIGHT

Seeing and Not Seeing in the Visual Arts

And yet—this is the contradiction essential to art—the supporting surface that we know to be actually there is not denied as flatness, and we feel this without feeling any the less the illusion that it is not there.
—Clement Greenberg, *The Collected Essays and Criticism, Vol. 3: Affirmations and Refusals, 1950–1956*

Humans have produced artifacts of all sorts, both useful and aesthetic, for tens of thousands of years. During Paleolithic times, beginning about 50,000 years ago, tools were produced not only with an eye for well-crafted axes, knives, needles, and so forth, but also with an eye for highly pleasing designs and shapes. Pendants and necklaces made of polished stones or shells had no use other than to render the wearer more attractive. And visual props, both shamanistic and sacral, were important for their symbolic as well as their aesthetic values. Like language, art is both product and producer of culture. And like language, art can be used both to conceal and to reveal aspects of our world. Highly ambiguous, pictorial art is subject to various takes: one beholder may see things in a work of art that another does not. Which take is "real"? According to some scholars following Plato's lead, neither one is real. In his day, Plato criticized the arts for rendering mere copies (e.g., artistic renditions of, say, a horse) of mere copies (e.g., a particular existing horse) of the Idea or Form (e.g., HORSE), *the* archetypal, universal, and objective Reality. Thus, the visual arts, according to Plato, triply obscure our knowledge of Reality by twice removing it through their two-fold copies and then by offering pleasurable diversions from our proper attention to that Reality. However, the particularity and ambiguity of visual art are what make it such a universally enjoyable enterprise for artists and beholders alike.

Plato and the problem of (not) "seeing" Reality aside, visual art, including "realistic" pictorial art, confronts us with a puzzle in more ways than one. Puzzles hide or veil an aspect of reality to which we remain oblivious unless and until we unveil or reveal it. This notion of unveiling or *alethea*, as it was known to the Greeks—of going beyond surface appearances—is the basis of any discovery. Like any puzzle such as a crossword, a cryptogram or a Sodoku, each of which requires some engagement of, and some struggle with, verbal or spatial skills before one attains a solution, pictures are puzzles requiring a beholder to engage visuocognitive skills before he or she can fully appreciate them as works of art. In my opinion, much of our sense of beauty, aesthetic engagement, interest, and delight at viewing a visual art object derives from its inherently puzzling ambiguity and complexity, to which each of us brings not only universal dispositions but also unique emotions, desires, and expectations that enrich the object's contextual space.

Let's begin with the bare facts of concealment and ambiguation in vision before we see how they apply to the perception of art. In Chapter 4 we noted how such animals as tree frogs use natural camouflage to visually "merge" themselves with their surrounding surfaces and thus to conceal themselves from predator and prey. Octopi and cuttlefish can additionally eject a dark dye that acts as a mask to render them invisible to a pursuing predator. Camouflage

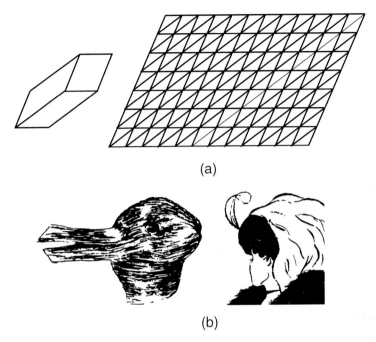

(a)

(b)

Figure 8.1. (a) An example of how a figure embedded in a larger complex array can fail to be seen. (b) Examples of ambiguous stimuli that can result in bistable percepts; here one of two possible percepts is perceived at any one time, while the other is not perceived.

and masking are two forms of concealment. In Chapter 5 we noted that selective masking can impair visual object recognition and that ambiguous figures can each be seen only one way at any time.

Figures 8.1 and 8.1b, respectively, present examples of visual concealment and ambiguity. On the left of Figure 8.1a is a two-dimensional depiction of a three-dimensional solid with quadrangular faces. Several copies of it also exist in the reticular display on the right of Figure 8.1a. However, any one of these copies is hidden or masked from easy view because the reticulation (a) acts as "noise" to the "signal" corresponding to each of the possible

copies, and (b) tends to be perceptually organized as a flat tessel-
lated pattern, thus counteracting the organization of a three-
dimensional percept. The illustration on the left of Figure 8.1b
can be seen as a duck or a rabbit; that on the right can be seen as the
as a young woman or a crone. Note that when one version is seen,
the other is not. Like the images shown in Figure 5.9, they again
illustrate the principle of flip-flop blinding and exemplify the type
of visual puzzles that have fascinated and delighted me, and no
doubt many a reader, ever since childhood.

NOT SEEING WHAT IS THERE

In the prior chapter, I noted that visuospatial imagery aided
mathematician Benoit Mandelbrot's discovery of fractal geometry.
Up to the time of their discovery a few decades ago, the mathematical order underlying natural fractal patterns was masked by
their irregular, less than orderly, appearance. We here have a case
of visual and cognitive masking, of not seeing the "signal" of the
structure embedded in the "noise" of the manifest irregularities. In
the 1950s, several decades before the discovery of fractal geometry,
the artist Jackson Pollock experimented with a series of drip
paintings, one of which is depicted in Figure 8.2. By the looks of
it, the painting depicts nothing but visual irregularity and chaos.
Yet it has an underlying structure that mimics one found in nature.
The structure is fractal. The physicists Richard Taylor, Adam
Micolich, and David Jonas have recently analyzed the fractal
dimensions of the drip paintings that Pollock issued between the
early 1940s and the early 1950s, and they compared them to
photographic images of natural scenes such as those of forests,
lightning patterns, clouds, land, mountainscapes, and so on. The
average fractal dimension of these images of natural scenes was
about 1.7. Pollock's earliest drip paintings had a fractal dimension

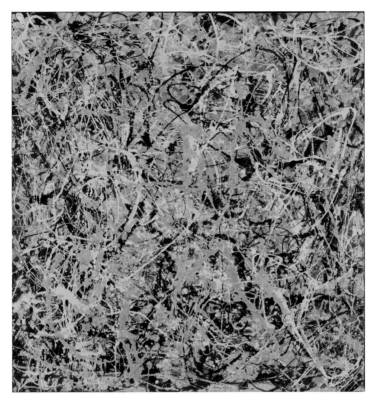

Figure 8.2. Pollock, Jackson (1912–1956)

© Artists Rights Society, New York. *Number 4*, 1949. Oil, enamel, and aluminum paint with pebbles on cut canvas, on composition board. 90.2 × 87.3 cm (35½ × 34⅛ in). The Katharine Ordway Collection. 1980.12.6; Yale University Gallery, New Haven, Connecticut; Photo credit: Yale University Art Gallery / Art Resource, New York.

of about 1.4. Two interesting features characterized Pollock's later drip paintings. First, progressively later drip paintings tended to have progressively higher fractal dimensions, and by the early 1950s the fractal dimension of his drip paintings approached the value found in photographic images of natural scenes. Second, around

1950 there was a clear outlier, a painting that did not follow this trend. It had a fractal dimension of 1.9, significantly higher than 1.7. He destroyed this painting. I conjecture that he noted something not quite right or pleasing with it; his subsequent drip paintings reverted to the lower fractal dimension of 1.7.

How do we explain these phenomena? I think the following, also noted by Taylor and his colleagues, gives a very plausible explanation. Pollock, like many painters, was a keen observer of the natural world. His visual system implicitly processed nature's fractal structures and established a mental representation that acted as an adaptive "filter" with a fractal dimension set point equal to 1.7. His evolving drip paintings were compared against this set point. Although the fractal dimensions of his initial paintings were substantially lower than this set point, the later ones progressively approached it, except for the 1950 outlier. Art historians and critics tend to classify these paintings as abstract expressionism. However, I take his drip paintings to exemplify additionally a concrete realism in so far as they portray the real but perceptually implicit, hidden fractal dimension of natural scenes.

Although Pollock's technique shows that nature's hidden structures can be implicitly portrayed in terms of a painting's features, the hiding of a painting's features or objects often is a very explicit, deliberate artistic device. In his book *Why Are Our Pictures Puzzles?*, the art historian James Elkins amply illustrates how artists have made use of masking and ambiguating techniques to accomplish such concealment. Some pictorial puzzles are rather obvious because artists have deliberately exploited and explored well-known optical techniques or perceptual phenomena either to make the images more difficult to see or to introduce ambiguation. Others require a vast stretch of the visual imagination in order to "see" the objects in them that some observers claim are "hidden." One example of a cleverly hidden message appears in Figure 8.3, the

Figure 8.3. Upper panel: Al Hirschfeld's cartoon drawing of *The Grateful Dead.*
Lower panel: Details of the images of Jerry Garcia (left) and Phil Lesh (right); the name
NINA appears in their hair.

artist Al Hirschfeld's cartoon of the Grateful Dead, in which he has hidden his daughter's name, NINA, in the hair of two of the band members. This was a typical flourish in many Hirschfeld cartoons, and finding the name encrypted in their linear contours adds to their visual pleasure—a two-for-one visual delight, a fresh motif embedding a new NINA surprise. Another example of visual encryption appears in Michelangelo's *Last Judgment* pane of the Sistine Chapel. It contains a facial image (see Fig. 8.4), which according to some art historians is Michelangelo's self-portrait.

But discovering faces hidden in art or nature is so common an occurrence that some may be apt to see them in everything. Humans are a highly social species to which faces communicate powerful social signals. From our first to our last breaths, we arguably encounter human faces more often than any other types of visual object. Recall that our brains have an area dedicated more or less to the visual processing of faces. For these reasons, we readily tend to see faces in clouds, trees, underbrush, metallic reflections, stellar constellations, and just about anything that even remotely conforms to one or more major features of a face. In his book, Elkins mentions how several art historians endorsed a claim, originally made by another historian, that faces are visible in Albrecht Dürer's sketches of pillows shown in Figure 8.5. To me, this is a real stretch. I might see a noselike protuberance or what looks like an eye here and there, but next to the crumpled pillows what I most easily see are crevasses in hilly or mountainous terrain or simply abstract topological manifolds. Perhaps my inability to see the faces is due to the fact that I suffer from some sort of misanthropy, a stunted imagination, or a lack of sophisticated appreciation of artworks.

Dürer's sketches and paintings are known for their realistic representational quality. Some of them, like *The Large Turf*, are astoundingly rich in form and color detail; they resemble a

Figure 8.4. Michelangelo Buonarroti (1475–1564), *Saint Bartholomew*, detail of *Last Judgment*. Sistine Chapel, Vatican Palace, Vatican State. St. Bartholomew displays his flayed skin, on which is what is believed to be Michelangelo's self-portrait.

Photo credit: Scala / Art Resource, New York.

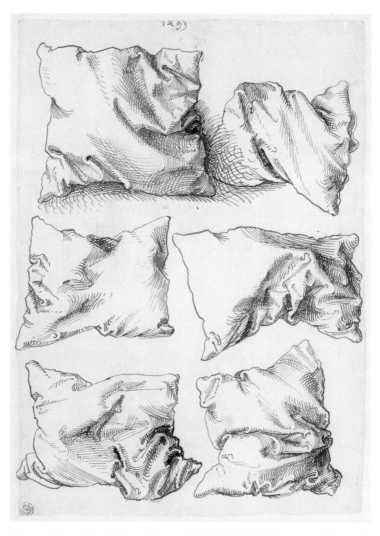

Figure 8.5. Albrecht Dürer (German, 1471–1528), *Six Pillows*, pen and brown ink, 10 15/16 × 7 15/16 in (27.8 × 20.2 cm).

The Metropolitan Museum of Art, Robert Lehman Collection, 1975 (1975.1.862); image © The Metropolitan Museum of Art.

high-resolution photograph and match any 20th-century photorealistic paintings. Such realistic images depend in large part on mastery of perspective, the technique and convention of rendering representations of realistic three-dimensional (3-D) scenes on a two-dimensional (2-D) surface. Perspective techniques were known in the classical era to Greek and Roman artists but subsequently fell into disuse. Rediscovered during the Renaissance, perspective exploits central projective geometry whereby points on the surfaces of 3-D objects and scenes map onto a 2-D image plane. A consequence of central perspective transformations is that parallel lines in the object space are not always mapped onto parallel lines in the image plane. Examples of such 2-D images are shown in Figure 8.6a, which depicts the same door totally shut and at three stages of opening. Notice that the 2-D images of the same rectangular door are trapezoidal, with progressively greater compressions along the horizontal image dimension as the door opens more widely. An alternate way of understanding central perspective is illustrated in Figure 8.6b, which presents an ovoid from two perspectives, the central projection points C_1 and C_2. From position C_1, one views the ovoid object sideways along a shallow angle; from position C_2, one views it head-on at an orthogonal angle. The object projection to C_1 and C_2 passes through two respective image planes. Image plane 1 is orthogonal to the object plane (bisecting the object lengthwise), while image plane 2 is parallel to the object plane. Note that the 2-D projection of the object on to image plane 2 renders an elliptical image, while the 2-D projection in image plane 1 renders a compressed circular image. Two artists positioned at C_1 and C_2, respectively, would sketch a circular and an elliptical outline of the same ovoid object on surfaces parallel to image planes 1 and 2.

Compressions or foreshortenings such as those shown in Figure 8.6 comprise one of several 2-D pictorial "cues" for the perception of depth. A crafty artist can invert the compressive

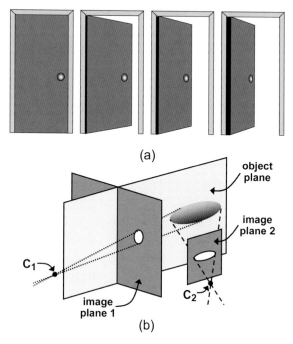

Figure 8.6. (a) Depictions of the same door at three stages of opening. (b) Schematic of how an ovoidal object projects onto two image planes as either a circle (image plane 1) or an ellipse (image plane 2).

transformation to yield anamorphically stretched 2-D images of 3-D objects. When viewed head on, the image is often unrecognizable; however, when viewed at shallow angles, the image reveals a recognizable object or scene. The contemporary artist Julian Beever has exploited anamorphic techniques in many of his delightful sidewalk drawings. Especially delightful and humorous are images of his pavement drawing entitled *Swimming-Pool in the High Street*, photographed from two viewpoints. The anamorphic and nonanamorphic images can be viewed at his website, http://users.skynet.be/J.Beever

under/wrongview.htm and/swim.htm, respectively. The former photo image taken from one side of the sidewalk sketch shows the stretched, distorted version of the swimming pool scene. The latter photo image, taken from the opposite side, shows how the distortions, when compressed and normalized due to a perspective, yield an image of an attractive blonde bather. To emphasize the normalized anamorphic illusion, the latter photo image also shows the artist trying to dip his right foot into the pool. Such anamorphic techniques have been used in art for millennia, but they became particularly popular during the late 16th and early 17th century, marking the transition from the late Renaissance to the Baroque period. One of the characteristics typifying the Baroque style of visual art is the twofold or ambiguous view. As Shakespeare wrote in *Richard II*:

> Like perspectives, which, rightly gaz'd upon
> Shew *nothing but confusion*; ey'd awry
> Distinguish *form*. [italics mine]

These lines capture the fascination with the double take exploited by perspective techniques and transformations current during Shakespeare's lifetime.

In contrast to their use in Beever's humorous pavement sketches, anamorphic distortions can be put to use in a more serious vein to render weightier themes. An example shown in Figure 8.7 is Hans Holbein's *The Ambassadors*, painted in 1533. Our eyes are taken naturally to the two bearded and stately men, Jean de Dinteville on the left and Georges de Selve on the right, each richly dressed in accordance with their ambassadorial status. Both men were diplomatically and personally involved in the confusions and intrigues of post-Reformation politics. Their gaze and posture are relaxed but straightforward and firm as they frame the sundry instruments and appurtenances befitting the learned, cultured,

Figure 8.7. Holbein, Hans the Younger (1497–1543), *Jean de Dinteville and Georges de Selve (The Ambassadors)*, 1533. Oil on oak, 207 × 209.5 cm. Bought 1890 (NGI314). National Gallery, London, Great Britain. At the bottom of the figure is shown a normalized version of the skull produced by compressing or foreshortening the anamorphic version.

© National Gallery, London / Art Resource, New York.

and confident persons of the late Renaissance that they were. Yet, the setting they occupy appears restricted to entry; it is *their* rightful space. An odd elongated object at the bottom of the painting—an obstacle hovering like a strange smear above the floor—disinvites others from entering into their space. Closer inspection reveals that the object is an anamorphic (stretched) image of a skull, a *memento mori*, reminding us of the worm in the fruits of the two ambassadors' worldly success. On even closer inspection, only possible when viewing the painting "live" in London's National Gallery, the large anamorphic skull resembles the skull on a barely visible badge pinned obliquely to the rim of Dinteville's beret. In other *vanitas* paintings of that period, human skulls usually were explicitly and prominently included as an object of contemplation on the transience and mortality of creation. Here, however, Holbein has deliberately rendered the presence of the skulls at a hidden, implicit level; one by its small size, the other by its anamorphic distortions. To see the larger skull more clearly, look at the painting from an extreme lower left perspective, akin to assuming the vantage point C_1 in Figure 8.6. It sometimes helps additionally to view the image of the skull through a tube of rolled up paper, so as to isolate it from the rest of the painting.

Several years ago, I heard that commercial artists use similar anamorphic techniques to render a double message in advertisements: an explicit, overt message of comfort and well-being and an implicit, hidden message of threat. Why these conflicting emotional messages? Threats produce physiological arousal and elicit fear; both moderate, attention-getting arousal and the accompanying fear (of being unpopular, rejected, unloved, ill, or of otherwise missing out on life) can be powerful motivating forces in advertising. According to drive reduction theories of human motivation, assuaging such implicitly or unconsciously aroused fear by the explicit promise of well-being can be a very rewarding and,

Figure 8.8. *Slave Market with Apparition of the Invisible Bust of Voltaire,* 1940. Oil on canvas, 18¼ × 25 ¾ in.

© Salvador Dalí. Fundación Gala-Salvador Dalí (Artists Rights Society), 2006. Collection of the Salvador Dali Museum, Inc. St. Petersburg, FL, 2006.

thus, a very effective advertising ploy. The basic message: WATCH OUT! What you can't see might harm you; and what you do see will help you.

Another artistic technique known to vision researchers and perception psychologists frequently appears in Salvador Dali's surreal paintings, such as his *Slave Market with Apparition of the Invisible Bust of Voltaire* (see Fig. 8.8). In fact, throughout his life, Dali's works kept pace with developments in vision research. Like the ambiguous shapes shown in Figure 8.1b, this painting is an exercise in evoking the type of multistable perceptual phenomena investigated by gestalt psychologists during the first half of the

20th century. In one version, the focal point of the painting can be perceived as two women, side by side, entering a spacious room through an arched entryway. In the alternate version, one perceives a bust of an elderly, grinning Voltaire. The upper white area of the arch defines his forehead and hairline, the heads of the two dark-haired women or nuns comprise his brows and sunken eyes, and their white chest bibs define the crest of his nose and his upper cheek. The additional white area below the bibs defines his chin.

Over the past two decades, I have shown a slide of the painting to my undergraduate perception classes. A good number of students, while readily seeing the nuns entering through the arched doorway, have failed to see Voltaire's bust at exposure durations of up to 2 minutes, even when its delineating features are pointed out to them. At times even I, a seasoned observer of such phenomena, am baffled at not seeing the hidden objects in analogous displays that initially appear like irregular arrays of light and dark blotches until, a good while later and with a good bit of luck, the "gestalt switch" or "Aha! moment" occurs and I finally see the meaningful objects. As mentioned in Chapter 6, such failures of perceptual gestalt reorganization of an invariant visual stimulus resemble the failures of object recognition in some of the visual associative agnosias.

Another way of looking at the perceptual perseveration of the part-dominated version of multivalent displays—and thus at the blindness to their other, holistic version—is in terms of the parts and local detail in a display (e.g., the nuns and their habits in Fig. 8.8) acting as masks to suppress perception of the global gestalt whole (Voltaire's smiling visage). Research on visual perception tends to support this interpretation. From July 1973 until August 1974, I had the pleasure of collaborating with visual scientist Bela Julesz at the Bell Laboratories in Murray Hill, New Jersey, on a number of vision research projects. In 1972, he had copublished with Charles Stromeyer an influential paper on what

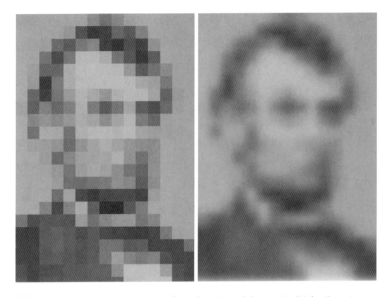

Figure 8.9. Left: Block image of Abraham Lincoln's portrait. Right: Same image with higher spatial frequencies filtered out.

is known as spatial frequency masking. Higher spatial frequencies convey the detailed spatial information in a visual display, such as its sharp edges and smaller features, whereas the intermediate and lower ones tend to convey the progressively coarser and more global aspects in a display. Just before my arrival, Leon Harmon and Bela published a paper on the perceptual difficulties posed by "block" images, akin to that shown in the left panel of Figure 8.9, and described how those difficulties might be related to the suppressive masking effects investigated earlier by Charles and Bela. By removing or filtering out the higher spatial frequencies that masked the neighboring lower ones, they demonstrated how the visibility of the underlying global structure of a face, shown in the right panel of Figure 8.9, was allowed to emerge.

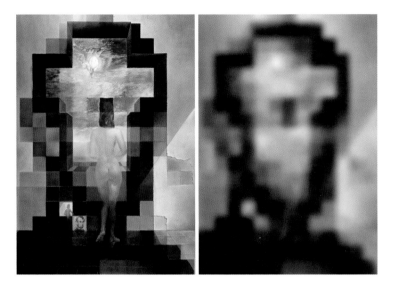

Figure 8.10. Left panel: *Gala Contemplating the Mediterranean Sea Which at Twenty Meters Becomes the Portrait of Abraham Lincoln - Homage to Rothko* (Second version), 1976. Oil on canvas, 75½ × 99¼ in.

Right panel: An image of the painting with high spatial frequencies filtered out.

© Salvador Dalí. Fundación Gala-Salvador Dalí (Artists Rights Society), 2006. Collection of the Salvador Dali Museum, Inc. St. Petersburg, FL, 2006.

However, it turns out that blurring of such images has nearly the same effect as selectively removing the higher spatial frequency content from them. For instance, if you are far sighted, remove your glasses and hold the block image close to you so that it is out of focus. As noted in Chapter 7, another way to eliminate the details in an image and thus mimic the effects of blur is to squint your eyes nearly shut. Try it on another one of Salvador Dali's paintings, shown in the left panel of Figure 8.10. This painting again is a deliberate exercise in incorporating the results of vision research. The block portrait of Lincoln in the painting and its miniature inset at the lower left, in fact, are facsimiles of the Lincoln portrait used in the 1973 study reported by Leon Harmon and Bela Julesz.

The multivalent ambiguity of Leonardo da Vinci's paintings has also occasioned a long history of studied commentary. His most famous painting, the *Mona Lisa*, is known for its enigmatic quality, expressed most notably in her *sfumatoed* glance and smile. The author Dan Brown, best known for his recent historical fiction, *The Da Vinci Code,* has sensationalized this quality—perhaps out of proportion—by seeing patterns of code encrypted in the *Mona Lisa* and the *Last Supper* that many viewers—including I myself—fail to see (or believe, even when they "see" them). That many readers regard Brown's theses as historically convincing bespeaks the power of fiction and ought not cause wonder, given the fact that a large number of people, including prominent public figures, do their reality checks by consulting readers of palms, tea leaves, astrological charts, and so on. But then to paraphrase the 17th-century English philosopher Francis Bacon, people prefer to see and believe what they wish to be true.

"SEEING" WHAT IS NOT THERE

I have used the quotes in "seeing" to make a point. There are very many ways in which we have perceptions of objects or of their properties that have no counterpart in external, objective reality; in other words, they are not *there*. Visual or "optical" illusions, two of which are shown in Figure 8.11, yield percepts for which there are no physical, external counterparts. On the left is shown the famous Müller-Lyer illusion, and on the right the less well known, but equally effective, Ebbinghaus illusion. To most people, the two vertical shafts in the Müller-Lyer illusion appear to have different lengths, the left one longer than the right one, when in fact they are

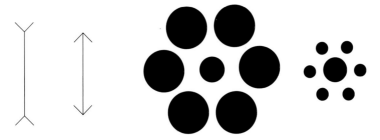

Figure 8.11. Left: The Müller-Lyer illusion. Right: The Ebbinghaus illusion.

equally long. The two inner circles in the Ebbinghaus illusion appear to be of different diameters, the left one smaller than the right one, when in fact they have identical diameters. And so on with other such visual illusions. Here, externally existing objects give rise to misperception of one of their properties. In hallucinations, the misperception is even more radical, having no external, visual object to perceive, although the hallucination can be very convincing regarding its external reference. In the following discussion, I will not talk about these kinds of hallucinatory "seeing" but rather about another kind that is part and parcel of everyday, normal perception. Because it is so mundane and taken for granted, it is a more subtle way of seeing what is not there.

Visual cognition is the end product of a complex process that depends as much on sensory registration of external stimuli (the information content in the world) as on the activation of internal representations (the brain's information content residing in its adaptive programs, stored concepts, and memories). This was the premise adopted in discussions of visual agnosias in Chapter 6. And it makes for an interesting feature of vision that flies below our cognitive radar during our mundane commerce and concerns with objects and events in the world. To wit, we visually cognize much more than what is presented to us through the sensory registration of external stimuli.

Some perception psychologists adopt a position of direct realism, claiming that all the information required for visual cognition resides in the external world and is given to us directly through the senses. Clearly, I find this approach limiting, since it (a) fails to do justice to the huge amount of information residing in both the genetically endowed and the adaptively modifiable functional architecture of the brain and thereby (b) forecloses research on a large part of visual cognition. As a vision scientist, I adopt a position of indirect or hypothetical realism. We do know the world not only via the bottom-up information picked up by our sensory apparatus but also via top-down processes akin to hypothesis generating that are adaptively updated by reality checks on whether the bottom-up information matches or mismatches the top-down hypothesis. In case of a match, the information generated by the top-down inference process can serve to fill in the informational gaps in the bottom-up information; in case of a mismatch, the inference must be altered by generating a different hypothesis. Examples of such a mismatch process were discussed in Chapter 5.

From this theoretical standpoint, one of the most interesting aspects of visual cognition is the existence of illusory contours and what is known as object constancy or object permanence. Related to this concept are the notions of modal and amodal perceptual completion. In modal completion, one sees contours where there are no physical edges defined by luminance or chromatic (wavelength) differences. To vision scientists, these are known as *modal illusory contours*. Examples are shown in Figure 8.12. In the upper left is the Kanisza triangle, named after the Italian psychologist who constructed this illusory figure. The three black "Pac-Men" elements and the three outlined angles are aligned in such a way that

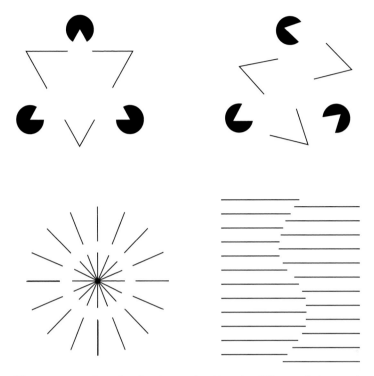

Figure 8.12. Examples of images, produced by using different techniques, each yielding the perception of illusory contours. The perception of illusory contours are due to modal contour completion.

most observers see an illusory white triangle—much like a real cutout of a white triangle—covering three black disks and an outlined triangle. Moreover, most observers "see" the straight contours of the triangle in the empty region between the Pac-Men. However, as we rotate the three Pac-Men and outlined angles in different directions by 30°–60° (shown in the upper right of Fig. 8.12), the illusory triangle and its modal contours are no longer seen. Many other ways of constructing modal illusory contours exist, including the two additional examples shown in the lower panels of the figure. In all such examples, modal contour completion occurs in objects perceived to be occluders of other objects or elements.

Let us now turn to object constancy and amodal completion. Suppose I ask that you give me your watch and I cover it with one of three inverted cups. Now I ask you to find your watch. To you this is a no-brainer. Although the watch in no longer directly available to you via visual registration, it remains indirectly available to you via temporarily stored visual information. Without deep deliberation, you know that the watch lies underneath the particular cup, despite your not being able to see it. This knowledge of object constancy is based on a lifelong fund of experiences. Humans develop it shortly after birth and of course retain and confirm it in countless experiences thereafter.

Consider an infant sitting in front of a toy train set that includes a tunnel. Now place an interesting object, say, a blue toy clown, in the train's freight car. As the train passes into the tunnel, the infant's eyes will "track" the train, and when it emerges in a timely manner, the infant will continue to track it and its cargo in an undisturbed way. In some sense the infant's perceptual system "expected" the train and cargo that entered and exited the tunnel to be identical. If, however, the experimental situation is set up so that a train carrying a different toy, say a brown teddy bear, emerges in a timely manner from the tunnel, the infant will show a startle or surprise response, typically via a change of facial expression. The infant's expectation based on object permanence was disconfirmed, since the bottom-up incoming data did not match the top-down expectation. In both cases, object permanence already was part of the infant's visuocognitive repertoire. This sort of startle or surprise reaction is retained in adulthood and in large part comprises the delight or shock we experience when one of our top-down inferences is disconfirmed by a magician's sleight-of-hand.

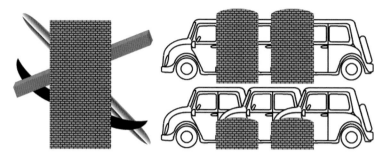

Figure 8.13. Three examples of amodal contour completion.

Amodal contour completion is a component of object constancy. For example, consider a person standing behind an opaque barrier that occludes everything from view except the person's legs just below the knees and the shoulders, neck, and head. Your experience is not of a person *sans* torso and upper legs, but rather of a whole person partly covered by the barrier. Your visuocognitive system knows that the contours defining the hips, waist, and lower torso of the whole person exist behind the barrier. This and the examples shown in Figure 8.13 illustrate *amodal completion of contours*. On the left of the figure, one has the visual impression that the contours of a number of straight and curved abstract objects exist behind each other and a visual barrier. In the bottom right panel of the figure, one gets the visual impression of three small cars, with each rightward displaced car partly occluding the immediate left one, and each of the two low barriers, in turn, partly occluding two cars at a time. Amodal contour completion occurs for occluded parts of all three cars. In contrast, the upper panel yields a very different effect. Here amodal contour completions tend to occur in such a way as to yield a visual impression of a limousine behind two higher barriers.

What is of interest here is that object constancy and its various manifestations are such an all-pervasive and cognitively "transparent" part of our daily visual experiences that we take their existence, like that of the air we breathe, for granted. However, if we take a more analytic attitude and consider carefully what is given to our visual sense when we look at a scene full of 3-D objects, we are struck with the fact that what is presented to the visual sense at any one time is only the "front" surface of the object, since only the light reflected from the surfaces facing us can reach our eyes. Given that, why are we not led to perceive, based on the "evidence of the senses," that the whole scene is merely a set of hollow 2-D facades or masks, like the props and stage scenes in many a Hollywood cinematic production? How, in our daily existences, do we visually know, without thinking about it, that what is in front of us is not a collection of 2-D fakes but real, solid 3-D objects?

I would argue that our visual systems have been educated, beginning shortly after birth, to the existence of solid objects in a 3-D world. Many objects are able to move on their own, many static ones can be manipulated and moved, and we can move around the ones that cannot be moved. In all three cases, in systematic fashion we are able to create a series of what the vision scientist David Marr has called "2½-D sketches" of these objects. This serial sampling of 2½-D sketches is complemented by our ability, once we learn to crawl and walk, to move around a solid object and visually acquire systematically changing 2½-D facets. From this rich commerce with our visual environment, the visual system eventually learns to automatically implement the "object completion" schema, which ends up rendering to our visuocognitive systems what Marr has called 3-D representations of objects or what we might call solid or volumetric object representations.

Figure 8.14. Left panel: Picasso, Pablo (1881–1973). *Guitar on Table*. Kunsthaus, Zurich, Switzerland.
Right panel: Picasso, Pablo (1881–1973). *Jacqueline*, 1960. Coll. Picasso, Mougins, France.
© Artists Rights Society, New York. Photo credit: Scala / Art Resource, New York.
© Artists Rights Society, New York. Photo credit: Scala / Art Resource, New York.

The upshot is that our visual cognitions are much more than what is given to our sense of sight via the light rays transmitted to our eyes. We visually "know" much more than we "see." This realization may have been a significant contributor to one of the major developments in 20th-century artistic styles, Cubism and its variants. As Picasso said pointedly, in response to a query about why he did not represent his scenes and objects more realistically or naturally, "I paint what I know, not what I see." The problem for Picasso and other Cubists was to render on 2-D canvases the 3-D structures of objects that our visuocognitive system knows. The solution, as shown in Figure 8.14, was to render on a single canvas several facets of an object side by side, in order to approximate the object's constancy as one moves around it. In that sense, one could argue that the Cubist style is actually more realistic than the representational style based on perspective techniques. While the latter offers only one viewpoint of an object, the former offers a sample of the many possible viewpoints of what we know to be the same (constant, nonchanging) object. Vision researchers call the representation of an object from a single viewpoint "viewer centered"; the latter object representation is called "object centered." Most entities we encounter visually are three dimensional and are represented in our visual cognition as object-centered three-dimensional structures. Is it any wonder that Cubism was based on a three-dimensional object, the cube, or that compared to Cubism, realistic representation is—at least to the avant-garde—so quaint as to be "square?" Notice, however, that Picasso's *Guitar on Table* (left panel), painted in 1915 shortly after the height of the Cubist movement, is rather flat and edgy compared to the more sinuous, busty *Jacqueline* (right panel), painted 45 years later.

More recently, such in-the-round artistic representation of objects, combining sharp edge with mellow curve, has also been a theme in several of David Hockney's paintings, two of which are depicted in Figure 8.15. In portraying the foreground objects, the chairs, Hockney uses curved, voluble representations against rectilinear, edgy background elements. Additionally, the chair shown in the left panel is painted in inverted perspective. Combined, these techniques render the dynamic transformations when viewing real three-dimensional objects such as chairs while moving around them. In such in-the-round viewing, the stream of visual consciousness flows over the many surfaces of an object yielding a succession of viewer-centered 2½-D representations, yet the 3-D, object-centered cognitive representation embraces what at any one moment in the stream and from any one perspective is not seen. Cubist artists and

Figure 8.15. Left panel: David Hockney, *The Chair* 1985; oil on canvas; 48 × 36 in. Right panel: David Hockney, *Two Pembroke Studio Chairs,* 1984; lithograph; edition: 98; 18½ × 22 in.

© David Hockney; Photo credit: Steve Oliver.
© David Hockney / Tyler Graphics Ltd.

Hockney attempt to disclose or reveal this greater reality that literally lies hidden from view behind any one visual take of the world that standard perspective techniques rely on.

HIDDENNESS INHERENT IN ART

Our visual takes of the world are determined not only by our physical but also by our conceptual topography. An artist's visual concepts and schemata no doubt differ noticeably from those of us who are visually less talented. For that reason, artists see or discover things that most of us overlook. This contributes in one way to art's inherent hiddenness: we simply cannot step behind the artist's eyeballs, and thus, we cannot see how and what the artist sees. The best we can do, with genuine surprise and wonder at times bordering on awe, is to delight in the artistic rendition of his or her view.

Figure 8.16. Magritte, René (1898–1967).
© Artists Rights Society, New York. *La Trahison des Images* (*Ceci n'est pas une pipe*), 1929. Oil on canvas,
60 × 81 cm. Los Angeles County Museum of Art, Los Angeles, CA. Photo credit: Banque d'Images,
ADAGP / Art Resource, New York.

However, art's hiddenness manifests itself in a much more mundane way. Pictorial art is inherently ambiguous and puzzling. The reason, as noted in the Clement Greenberg epigraph that began this chapter, is that a painting, drawing, or photograph is two things at once. It is a visual object in its own right, and it simultaneously serves a representational function. It is a thing and a depiction of things, a fact seriocomically pointed out in Réné Magritte's *La Trahison des Images* (see Fig. 8.16). Children as young as 2 years are aware of this dual nature of pictures. What contributes to the object nature of a work of art? A number of things, including the existence of a frame, the surface texture of a painting, the

Figure 8.17. del Caso, Pere Borrell (1835–1910). *Escapando de la Crítica* (*Escaping Criticism*), 1874. Oil on canvas, 72 × 62 cm.
© Banco de España, Madrid.

graininess of a photograph, and so forth. However, we see through this into a reality behind the frame, the texture, or the grain, much as we would see through the mesh of a screen door into a backyard flower garden. So, when viewing pictorial art, we typically are not focally aware of the work as an object but only of its contents, no

Figure 8.18. Pozzo, Andrea (1642–1709). *St. Ignatius in Glory*, ceiling fresco in the nave of the Church of San Ignazio. S. Ignazio, Rome, Italy.
Photo credit: Alinary / Art Resource, New York.

matter how realistic or surrealistic, sensorial or conceptual, or concrete or abstract those contents are. Indeed, this blindness can be so complete, particularly in trompe l'oeil art, as to trick (*tromper* in French) the viewer into believing that a 3-D window or vista is opening up before him.

Two examples of effective trompe l'oeil art are given in Figures 8.17 and 8.18. The first painting, entitled *Escaping Criticism*, by 19th-century Spanish artist Pere Borrell del Caso amusingly depicts a young lad climbing out of a picture frame toward the viewer. He is as much astonished at the view of the "real" world outside the (painted) frame of the picture as we are at the artful depiction of this illusory three-dimensional escape scene. The second painting, by the 17th-century Italian painter Fra Andrea

Pozzo, is a depiction, on the vaulted ceiling of the Church of St. Ignazio in Rome, of St. Ignatius entering heaven. When looking straight up from the center of projection below the ceiling, one has the vivid impression of the actual architecture of the church extending through the ceiling into the heavens above. This virtual-reality vista is made especially effective by the substantial viewing distance, which renders invisible the surface details, such as the paint's texture, cracks, and so on. These examples of trompe l'oeil art illustrate dramatically that for the most part, short of deliberately assuming an analytic attitude, we remain blind to the dual, surface versus scene, aspect of visual art.

A striking visual metaphor for this blinding can be found Andrea Mantegna's *Archers Shooting at Saint Christopher*, shown in the upper panel of Figure 8.19. Plumbing the historical depths of this metaphor could entail several book-length studies. In fact, the jacket cover of Michael Kubovy's book, *The Psychology of Perspective and Renaissance Art*, features a detail of the painting, shown in the lower panel of the figure. As noted previously, perspective is the technique of rendering a 2-D optic array that is nearly identical to that offered by a natural 3-D scene. It is based on geometric principles according to which rays of light converge on a central projection point, in this case, the pupil of the eye. A perspective painting can be considered as the embodiment of an imaginary image plane intersected by the rays of light as they pass, once reflected from the surfaces in the 3-D scene, to the convergence point. In the Mantegna painting, the arrow entering the eye stands for one such perspective ray entering the eye. Mantegna is saying that light, considered as a bundle of individual perspectival rays inter-secting an image plane, can blind the eye—itself a synecdoche for the entire act of vision and visual cognition— while simultaneously illuminating it. It is no coincidence that Fra Andrea Pozzo, when executing his painting on the ceiling of St. Ignazio, followed precisely

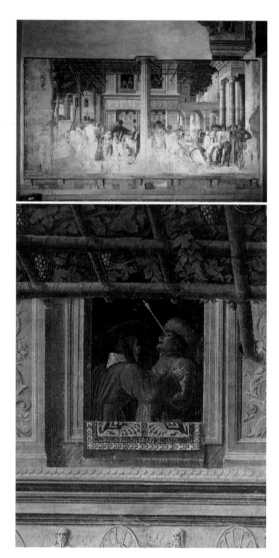

Figure 8.19. Upper panel: Mantegna, Andrea (1431–1506). *Martyrdom and Transposition of the Body of Saint Christopher.* Fresco, Ovetari Chapel. Chiesa degli Eremítaní, Padua, Italy.

Lower panel shows a detail of one of the arrows piercing the eye of an onlooker

Photo credit: Scala / Art Resource, New York.

the rules of perspective that confer to the eye of the viewer standing on the floor of the church the role of central projection point.

One can think of such perspectival representations as 2-D images true to 3-D reality or nature—as art substituting for nature. Or as Ernst Gombrich pointed out in his book *Art and Illusion*, they can be regarded as deceptive visual tricks that, rather than reveal nature, actually conceal and thus blind us to it. Nature and reality are richer than any take of them. This theme, as we saw, is captured in the works of painters like Picasso and Hockney. One tendency of 20th century art has been to render images increasingly abstract and conceptual. A single photograph-like image can activate highly familiar and concrete perceptual schemata that are also activated by natural or real-world scenes. Such activations, occurring thousands of times a day, are a routine and automatic feature of perception. For that reason, they tend to foreclose on any questioning of reality. On the other hand, nonrealistic, abstract, and conceptual arts, because they are not easily assimilated into ready-made perceptual schemata, force us either to suspend the dichotomy between art as object and art as representation, and thus to seek the message in the medium, or to ask questions, to seek meaning and reality behind and beyond images. The latter alternative powerfully brings to the forefront what Gombrich has called the "beholder's share," a share that, in the early 21st century, partakes of increasingly greater levels of cognitive sophistication.

NINE

Cognitive Blindspots
Bloopers and Blunders

*. . . cognitive illusions are the product of the demon of mental
facility. . .mental shortcuts [that] just happen to us, . . .that derive
from how we are made, and not from our gender, our culture, our
language, or our education.*

MASSIMO PIATELLI-PALMARINI, *INEVITABLE ILLUSIONS*

Despite much scientific progress, we do not fully know
what constitutes our human nature or how it interacts
with nurture to produce unique human beings. But we do know
two things: as human beings, we are naturally gifted and, alas,
naturally flawed. We are endowed with a brain capable of supporting perception and cognition to address mundane existential
needs and problems, we have language and speech to communicate
information, and we have technological and imaginative traditions
that we transmit from one generation to the next through training
and art. Those are our gifts. And our flaws? Many of course, but
one in particular is expressed in our many inabilities to think
clearly all the time. These are the cognitive blind spots, biases,
and illusions to which all humans are heirs, just as all humans are
prone to a host of perceptual biases and illusions of the sort
described in the previous chapter (see, e.g., Fig. 8.11).

The biologist Gunter Stent hypothesized that our perceptuo-cognitive biases may have been biologically inherited. Neurophysiological studies of cats and monkeys indicate that the functional architecture of the visual cortex disposes or biases these animals toward an initial cortical analysis of the visual world in terms of straight contours and lines of varying orientation. This disposition is given at birth, although, as noted in Chapter 4, it can be significantly influenced by environmental factors (i.e., nurture). By reasonably extrapolating to the human visual cortex, Stent argues that a similar innate disposition may have contributed to geometers' readily discovering the properties (theorems) of plane or Euclidean geometry while remaining cognitively blind for a long time (about 2,000 years) to those of non-Euclidean, for example, Riemannian, geometry. Conversely, he suggests that if the receptive fields of neurons of the human primary visual cortex had evolved to have a curvilinear rather than a rectilinear geometry, the principles of non-Euclidean spherical geometries might have been discovered before those of plane geometry. Because they are supported by strong intuitions or strongly ingrained premises, ingrained Euclidean biases are very difficult to override, even in highly rational minds like those of Immanuel Kant. His Euclidean concept of space was based on (read "biased by") what he considered to be a natural, a priori mode of intuition. So even in our attempts at a cool, dispassionate, and rational assessment of facts and truths, we are prone to biases, many of which are part of our natural inheritance.

Several years ago, while teaching an undergraduate course on critical thinking in psychology, I noticed an interesting phenomenon. On the one hand, my students were usually able to apply critical thinking successfully to various psychological research issues. On the other hand, as evidenced by their dismay at their test scores, many students were by and large overly confident about what they claimed to know and about how well they were able to think in a logically valid and bias-free manner. Their confident belief in their abundance of knowledge of critical thinking skills was an illusion or bias that—at least temporarily—blinded them to the less palatable recognition of how little they actually knew.

Detecting the flaw in a logical argument described in a test question is an example of a "cold" or affectless cognition, something akin to seeing the truth of the rule of association: $(a + b) \cdot c = (a \cdot c) + (b \cdot c)$. Even a properly programmed computer can blindly and affectlessly assess chess move options or prove mathematical theorems and thus in some sense "know" which move to choose or "recognize" the truth of a theorem. The notion of the primacy of cold cognition was in its heyday during the first half of the 20th century, when a philosophical movement known as logical positivism held that all meaningful and true statements must be—and therefore are—either empirically verifiable or logically provable. This strictly ruled out all other avenues to meaning or truth. Ironically, the logician Kurt Gödel countered this belief by proving that within a logically consistent system—even one as simple as the integer system—true and meaningful statements do exist that remain unprovable within that system. And though still questioned by many a philosophically inclined mind, at an experiential level there is indeed a realm of meaning beyond pure logic or observable fact. Stephen Hawking, one of the most cerebral of mathematical physicists, noted that his physical understanding of the cosmos left him rather cold. For something more fully meaningful, he preferred instead to turn to human companionship or to the music of Mozart. He preferred, in other words, the "hot" cognition of emotional experience.

Emotions were also in play in the dismay of my students who performed worse on their exams than they had expected. Seeing their own flaws (or virtues) or those of someone whom they love and admire typically causes a stir of "hot" cognition, the heat being provided by unpleasant emotions such as anxiety and anger (or pleasant ones such as joy and delight).

Both cold and hot cognitions are examples of what social psychologists and cognitive scientists regard as motivated cognitions. When appraising the logical or scientific validity of a claim or when considering the rational course of action to take in making, say, economic, decisions, we are motivated by the goals of achieving, *within the system of scientific logic and reason*, objective, accurate conclusions, in other words, scientific truths. When appraising ourselves and others, we are motivated additionally, and often primarily, by achieving a directional conclusion, that is, an achievement steered by a host of emotional and subjective factors that lie outside the realm of objective truth seeking and sometimes outside of our awareness. In the following chapter, we will briefly deal with the topic of hot cognitions and some of their biases and blind spots. For now let's get better acquainted with cold cognitions and some of the blindnesses afflicting them.

SOME FALLACIES AND BIASES IN COLD COGNITIONS

Thinking critically is important in problem solving, assessing risks and options in situations with limited choices, evaluating an argument's or a proof's validity, decision making, drawing probabilistic and statistical inferences, and so on. As examples, imagine yourself trading in the stock futures or precious-metal markets or deciding how to allocate your limited resources toward paying for your daughter's ongoing college education and her upcoming wedding. You will rely on critical thinking as you try to make the right choice about whether to buy or sell in the stock market and to pay for one or the other or all of your daughter's expenses. But most humans, like my students, are notoriously fallible in assessing these types of situations, despite confident claims to the contrary. Even in less uncertain situations in which there are clear-cut, correct answers or decisions, thinking can go awry. The human mind is like a tinker toy, built from various and separate parts that somehow interrelate in ways that do not guarantee neat and admirable outcomes of decisions or solutions to problems. So, as many cognitive scientists have shown in recent decades, we are prone to make errors in reasoning. Amos Tversky's research on a variety of problem-solving, risk-assessment, and decision-making situations and on the fallacies that can easily slip into the thinking process was particularly fruitful, as was his collaboration with Daniel Kahneman, winner of the 1996 Nobel Prize in Economics; their work addressed universal concerns and limitations related to rational thought and action.

Despite culture-specific variations, in every culture a person is often faced with choices between two or more mutually exclusive courses of action and therefore must assess risks, costs, and benefits and decide on a specific alternative. The choices may be trivial—for example, choosing which snack you can buy to satisfy your sweet-tooth problem when you have only small pocket change on you at a given moment—or very consequential—for example, deciding whether to see a doctor or to buy groceries to address your subsistence problems when you have only a monthly Social Security stipend. Solving problems, assessing risks, and making decisions depend, among other things, not only on adequate information and appropriate motivation but also on adequate information-processing (i.e., cognitive) capacities and strategies.

One *ideally* addresses a problematic or a choice situation first by becoming thoroughly familiar with the relevant facts of the situation—that is, by initially gathering as much information about it as possible. When all or most of the parts of the puzzle are at hand, the problem solving can commence. This is usually accomplished by narrowing an originally large space of possibilities, the so-called search space, by some processes of elimination until one homes in on a smaller subset of possible solutions. Depending on where one starts in such a search space, there are many approaches or paths to solving problems or to making decisions that can lead to a more or less satisfactory outcome.

The path leading to an insight is illustrated by the famous example of Archimedes who was asked to determine if a crown was made of pure gold or, in case the goldsmith cheated, of an alloy containing an additional and cheaper metal. Archimedes's solution arrived like a bolt out of the blue sky (Eureka! I've got it!). After struggling with this problem for some time, he "saw in a flash" (a) that a pound of gold can be contained in a smaller volume than can a pound of a cheaper and less dense metal such as copper, (b) that the volume of the crown can be measured by how much the water level rose in a container when the crown was submerged in it, and (c) that by comparing on a scale the weight of the crown to that of gold displacing the same volume, he could determine whether or not the crown was made of pure gold according to the following rule: If the scale is balanced, the crown is made of pure gold, but if the end of the scale holding the crown tips up, it is made of an alloy.

This was an ideal problem-solving situation: Archimedes arrived at his Eureka moment of insight because he had the time to construct a conjecture, to assess it, to ponder alternatives, to step back, reframe the problem, think "outside the box," and so on. But often our everyday approaches to problem solving are fraught with many possible shortcomings. Humans often must solve their problems or come to decisions on the fly; they simply cannot expend the time and effort to carefully analyze their problem-solving procedures or to exhaustively consider alternatives of action. Worse, humans are lazy; suffering from mental sloth, they do not want to expend the

required time and effort. In either case, readily available and automatically activated rules and intuitions are very often applied to
settings where careful and more time-consuming thinking is called
for. Some of these shortcut rules are algorithmic, following specific
steps in order to arrive at a solution. Others are heuristic, relying on
more or less reliable general rules of thumb or intuitions rather than
on highly reliable and specifiable steps. Unfortunately, as we shall
see, an algorithm may not be applicable to solving a given problem.
Measuring a man's shoe size by a standard algorithmic procedure is
not a way to assess his level of extraversion. Moreover, heuristics,
although more generally applicable, are not always valid. For
example, adhering to the intellectual sloth's automatically activated
rule of thumb, "When in doubt, take the path of least effort," is a
way to exacerbate rather than solve many a problem; on the other
hand, following the obsessive-compulsive personality's automatically activated rule of thumb, "Do it perfectly or don't do it at
all," is a way to become stuck in an overscrupulous and interminable
process of assessing alternative possibilities. Applying more
thoughtful and fruitful cognitive rules and procedures is effortful,
since they tax intellectual, imaginational, motivational, and attentional resources.

Both algorithmic and heuristic approaches can be fraught
with cognitive blind spots. In his book *Inevitable Illusions*,
Massimo Piatelli-Palmarini discusses these blind spots in
terms of cognitive illusions that mislead us in our problem-
solving and decision-making endeavors. Such illusions result
from defects in logical or deductive reasoning, from conceptual
nonsense or errors, and/or from a variety of cognitive biases. Of
the many logical fallacies and biases that cognitive scientists
have discovered can afflict reasoning, I will highlight just a few
potent examples from my own informal experiments and from
Piatelli-Palmarini's book.

An Illusion Based on First and Quick Impression Formation:
The Anchoring Effect

Imagine that I give one group of subjects the task of estimating, within 5 seconds, the product of the following multiplicative series, $2 \times 3 \times 4 \times 5 \times 6 \times 7 \times 8$. I give a second group of subjects the task of estimating, under the same time constraint, the product of the following series, $8 \times 7 \times 6 \times 5 \times 4 \times 3 \times 2$. The correct answer in either case is 40,320, which most subjects could compute given sufficient time. But given the time constraint, the estimate given by either group of subjects is usually smaller. Most of us are aware that the rule of commutation applies to simple arithmetic operations such as addition or multiplication: The ordering of the terms in addition or multiplication has no effect on the sum or the product. Hence, based on that rational rule alone, we would expect the two groups of subjects to yield roughly the same estimate—even if it is still off the mark. What is intriguing and unexpected from a purely logical standpoint, however, is that the first group typically renders an average estimate that is significantly smaller than the second group's average estimate. If you probe the subjects, they will acknowledge the validity of the rule of commutation. Yet this valid rule apparently is not invoked; instead, what more readily applies is an effect known as "anchoring." That is to say, the subjects in either group form an initial impression based on the first few terms of the multiplicative series—relatively low for the first group and relatively high for the second group—to which their extrapolated estimate of the entire series is anchored.

In my opinion, cognitive anchoring is an effect that has its analogue in certain stages of cognitive development explored by the Swiss psychologist Jean Piaget. According to his theory, formulated within an evolutionary and ontogenetic epistemology, young children progress through several stages of cognitive development, one of

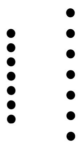

Figure 9.1. Vertical arrays of dots with equal numbers of dots but unequal spatial extents.

which is an early stage based on the formation of concrete sensorimotor schemata: that is, what the child "knows" at this stage is linked to his or her concrete sensory impressions. For instance, given two arrays of seven dots as shown in Figure 9.1, the young child will more likely than not say that the array on the right, which has a larger spatial extent than the left-hand array, has a larger number of dots. In this case, the potent *perceptual* impression based on the difference between the spatial extents of the two arrays of dots "takes hostage of" and thus dominates the child's cognition. Children will eventually outgrow this sensorimotor stage of cognitive development and progress to a stage where they will be able to counteract the automatic effects imposed by the sensory organization of visual stimuli and to abstract numerical magnitudes from perceptual or sensory magnitude. I believe that in adults anchoring is a bias based on analogously potent *conceptual* impressions that capture and dominate cognition. This cognitive bias also needs to be counteracted if we are to arrive at rationally based, objective assessments of factual states of affairs.

Illusions of Probabilistic Thinking
Our everyday world is full of maybes and uncertainties, requiring us to take courses of action or make choices that do not guarantee

successful attainment of goals. Often the best we can do is to assess probabilities and, based on such assessment, make decisions that we think are most likely to guarantee success. But here our thinking is fraught with a number of persistent and hard-to-recognize illusions, of which one of the most important is the *gambler's fallacy*. Here is an example of a problem that I at times pose to my undergraduate students when I introduce them to probabilistic concepts in my course on research methods. Suppose a fair coin with the typical head (H) and tail (T) sides, when tossed 10 times, yields the following outcome sequence: HTTHHHHHHH. Many students, when asked whether H or T is more likely to occur on the 11th toss, will say "T," and thus commit the gambler's fallacy. The intuition expressed in the heuristic, "If a coin is fair, the typical outcome of a string of tosses should be 50% heads and 50% tails," is reasonable. It is based on the valid assumption that in the long run, according to the law of large numbers, such a result is expected. Since the result of 10 tosses deviates from this probabilistic typicality, it makes apparent sense that the 11th toss is more likely to restore typicality by yielding a T. Careful thinking, however, will tell you that, if the coin indeed is fair, a T and H are equally likely outcomes (each with a likelihood of 50%) on any toss, regardless of the prior sequence of outcomes. Applying the law of large numbers to a small number such as 10 is one version of the gambler's fallacy.

Another version is based on the fact that our intuitive notion of randomness is quite different from reality. I have sometimes also engaged my students in the following exercise. I ask one group to flip a coin, say, 40 times and list the sequence of heads and tails. I ask another group to imaginatively flip coins and thus generate what they believe to be a random 40-toss sequence of heads and tails. One can fairly readily tell the differences between the two types of sequences by comparing the frequency with which certain strings are generated actually and imaginatively. In turns out that runs of head or tails, such as HHHHH or TTTTTT, are more frequent in the actual strings than in the imagined ones. Our easily accessible intuitive sense of randomness wrongly disallows long strings of the same outcome. We entertain a notion of a typical random sequence that simply does not correspond to the laws of probability.

Next, consider the following experiment, which begins with description of a fictional person:

> Betty is an active, physically fit person who likes the outdoors, has participated in several marathons, and enjoys traveling. In college she was an outstanding student, and her favorite courses were business management and English literature. She is married and has three children.

After reading this description, subjects are then asked to rank, in order of probability of being true, the following statements:

   a. Betty is a biochemist, and she prefers classical music.
   b. Betty is an interior designer.
   c. Betty works for a marketing firm.
   d. Betty's hobby is off-road biking.
   e. Betty is a media consultant.
   f. Betty works for a marketing firm and her hobby is off-road biking.
   g. Betty is a grandmother.

Notice that Statement f is a conjunction of Statements c and d. In an experiment such as this, most subjects will give Statement f a higher probability ranking than either Statement c or d. However, if you carefully think about it, the probability of any entity or person having two traits cannot exceed the probability of having one of the traits. By judging the conjunction of two states to be more probable than either of the two states alone, the subjects have committed a *conjunction fallacy*. They have taken a scenario that is more readily imaginable, that is, comes to mind more readily, to be more likely. Given the sketchy description of Betty, it just appears psychologically more typical for such a person to work for a marketing firm *and* to engage in off-road biking as a hobby than for such a person simply to work for a marketing firm or simply to enjoy off-road biking as a hobby. So we confuse ease of cognitive representation or typicality with likelihood.

Another fallacy in probabilistic thinking is what I call the *subjective-value fallacy*. Here, two equal or nearly equal outcomes are judged to have very different likelihoods of occurring because one of the outcomes has a higher subjective value attached to it than the other outcome. Typically, the bias is toward judging the more prized outcome as the rarer one and is supported by many cases of a valid inverse relation between value and rarity. No doubt there are more Honda Civics on the road than Porsches or Maseratis; more Casio sport watches on wrists than Cartier diamond watches, more sand dunes than oases in a desert, and so on. The subjective-value fallacy, in turn relying on the ancillary *tendency of overgeneralization*, plays out in many a game of chance. For example, I have found in my informal in-class experiments that in an imaginary game of straight poker, being dealt a royal flush (the Ace, King, Queen, Jack, and Ten of the same suit) is often judged—even by individuals who are familiar with the game—as a rarer event than being dealt a straight flush, such as the Two, Three, Four, Five, and Six of another suit. Similarly, being dealt an Ace and a Queen in blackjack, also known as twenty-one, is judged as rarer than being dealt a Seven and a Nine. But what if the game were sixteen instead of twenty-one? The Seven and Nine would be deemed the rarer pair than the then-unprized Ace and Queen.

Up to now, you likely have been able to understand or "see" the reasons behind these fallacies. However, there are fallacies of thinking that are real zingers, recognized with some difficulty even by bright minds. I include the following, somewhat arcane example adapted from Piatelli-Palmarini's book:

> Suppose we play a game of chance. On a table there are three boxes, each with a lid. I also have a generous stack of ten-dollar bills.
>
> Phase 1. You turn around so that you cannot see what I am doing. I put a ten-dollar bill in one of the three boxes and close the lids of all three. You now turn around, and I ask you to guess in which box I have placed a ten-dollar bill. If the game were over now and *if* you had guessed correctly, you, of course, would have won ten dollars. But the game does not end here. The game proceeds as follows.
>
> I know which two of the three boxes is empty (you of course don't know). I also know your initial choice and whether you picked the box containing the ten-dollar bill or one of the two empty boxes. If you picked the box containing the ten-dollar bill, I open the lid to one of the two empty boxes; however, if you picked one of the two empty boxes, I open the lid of the other empty box. In both cases you discover only that, of the two remaining closed boxes, one is definitely empty. Hence, you also know that the ten-dollar bill is either in the still-closed box you initially chose or else in the other still-closed box.
>
> Phase 2. At this point I give you the chance to stay with the closed box of your first choice or to switch your choice to the other closed box.

And now, here is the problem for you to solve: If we were to repeat this game, say, 200 times, would you win more money by sticking, in each game, to your first choice or by switching your choice?

If you have arrived at the correct answer for the right reasons, congratulations are due for your "Eureka!" experience (merely guessing correctly does not qualify as a right reason). However, similar to my reasoning when I first read this problem, your initial thought might be, "Well, there now are only two possibilities left, either the closed box that I initially chose contains the ten-dollar bill or else the other remaining closed box does. At this point, these two possibilities are equally likely. Hence, either strategy is equally likely to pay off, in other words, either decision has a 0.5 probability of paying off. Therefore, I might just as well stick with the initial choice as switch my choice each time the game is played." Doesn't it make intuitive sense that if two closed boxes remain, only one of which contains the ten-dollar bill, either box will be as likely to contain the payoff as the other, and that, therefore, in the long run it really does not matter if one always stays with the initial choice of boxes or always switches to the other or in each game flips a coin to decide whether or not to switch?

The answer is: No, it does not make sense, and it really does matter which of the two remaining boxes you chose. It turns out that the best strategy is to always switch choices. If this *seems* utterly counterintuitive, know that it *is* utterly right. As Piatelli-Palmarini explains,

> Suppose for instance, that your original choice was the right one; then when I open my empty box, for you to switch will *certainly* (not just probably) penalize you [you will be *plus* $0 rather than *plus* $10]. If, on the other hand, your first choice was an empty box, you will *certainly* (not just probably) gain by switching [you will be *plus* $10 rather than *plus* $0]. We have gained a little security. Let's use that. How often do you think your choice will be correct (and thus *necessarily* penalized if you switch)? One in three times. And how often will you choose an empty box (and thus be *necessarily* better off switching)? Two times out of three. [p. 164]

I am going to elaborate on this explanation in the following way:

Suppose for instance, that your original choice was the right one; then when I open my empty box, for you *not* to switch will *certainly* (not just probably) *reward* you [you will be *plus* $10 rather than *plus* $0]. If, on the other hand, your first choice was an empty box, you will *certainly* (not just probably) *lose* by switching [you will be *plus* $0 rather than *plus* $10]. We have gained a little security. Let's use that. How often do you think your choice will be correct (and thus *necessarily* rewarded if you don't switch)? One in three times. And how often will you choose an empty box (and thus be *necessarily* worse off not switching)? Two times out of three.

Therefore, using the switch strategy in every game (with a probability of 1) in the long run yields the following expected payoff for each game: $(0)[(\frac{1}{3})(+\$10) + (\frac{2}{3})(+\$0)] + (1)[(\frac{1}{3})(+\$0) + (\frac{2}{3})(+\$10)] = +\$6.67$. So over 200 games, you very likely would have won somewhere around $1,333. In contrast, using the stick strategy in every game (with a probability of 1) in the long run yields the following expected value for each game $(1)[(\frac{1}{3})(+\$10) + (\frac{2}{3})(+\$0)] + (0)[(\frac{1}{3})(+\$0) + (\frac{2}{3})(+\$10)] = +\$3.33$. So over 200 games, you very likely would have won somewhere around $667. On the other hand, if you flip a coin in each game to decide (with a probability of $\frac{1}{2}$) to switch and (with an equal probability of $\frac{1}{2}$) to not switch, the expected value for each trial is $(\frac{1}{2})[(\frac{1}{3})(+\$10) + (\frac{2}{3})(+\$0)] + (\frac{1}{2})[(\frac{1}{3})(+\$0) + (\frac{2}{3})(+\$10)] = +\$5.00$. So over 200 games, you very likely would have won somewhere around $1,000, falling between the expected values of the always-switch and the always-stick strategies. In fact, for any other overall strategy that allows some, but not all, of the games to be played with the stick option, the expected payoff after 200 games is always somewhere between $667 and $1,333, but never equal to either. So, with the goal of maximizing payoff, the optimal strategy is to switch in every game played. If you still don't understand the reason for the switching, as opposed to the sticking, strategy, well then you have not had that illuminative "Aha!" experience. Go over the above reasoning and examples again, perhaps at a later time. As the Hungarian-American mathematician, George Polya, pointed out (and as many of us might have experienced on our own), sometimes solving a problem benefits from a period of "incubation," in which you step back from and simply let go of the problem.

There are many more probability illusions that Piatelli-Palmarini discusses, and the interested reader can go to his book for a fuller appreciation of the many ways we fail to think correctly in situations offering uncertain outcomes.

Illusions of Nonprobabilistic Thinking

There are also fallacies of nonprobabilistic or deterministic thinking even when the outcome is 100% certain. As an example that illustrates how one can arrive at a wrong conclusion by applying an inappropriate algorithm, consider the following problem that I have posed to a number of people:

> A woman drives 120 miles from point A to point B at a speed of 80 miles an hour and returns from point B to point A driving at a speed of 20 miles an hour. What is her overall average speed?

To many readers this problem is reminiscent of similar ones posed in their high school algebra texts. A snap but incorrect answer that many people give is 50 miles an hour, the average of 80 and 20. In this situation, averaging is actually an apt procedure. But the (long-forgotten) specific algebraic rule or algorithm to apply in this case is to average not on the basis of the proportion of total distance traveled during each leg of the trip (0.5 for both legs), which yields the incorrect answer of 50 miles per hour, but rather on the basis of the proportion of total time (0.2 and 0.8 for the first and second leg, respectively), which yields the correct answer of 32 miles hour.

Akin to the cases of inattentional blindnesses of vision discussed in Chapter 5, the individuals who gave the "quick-and-dirty" answer were distracted by the explicitly given but irrelevant distance information, thus disregarding the larger context only implicitly containing the relevant time information. Again this illustrates that in some cases thinking, like attentively scanning the visual world, must be slow, cautious, and effortful; one must first think about how to frame the problem within the entire context before trying to solve it, but this requirement often goes against the easy grain.

In some intellectual disciplines, such as mathematics, valid deductive reasoning is the narrow but sure path to determining the truth of propositions such as theorems. As in mathematical propositions, many other propositions begin with a premise, "if X" or "given X," and end with a conclusion, "then Y." Let's take a common national and male stereotype as an example: *If you are an Italian man, then you are a great lover.* Let's also assume that we know perfectly well what a great lover is, so there is no problem of differentiating a great lover from an average or poor lover. Now, test the validity of this stereotype by interviewing one of the following:

1. Italian men.
2. non-Italian men.
3. great lovers.
4. nongreat (poor and average) lovers.

Exercising which of these four interviewing options would be most helpful toward achieving your assigned goal? If you are like nearly all other persons tested on problems of this sort, you would be most likely to choose Option 1, less likely to go for Option 3, less still for Option 2, and least likely for Option 4. In choosing Option 1, you will have made a good choice, since interviewing Italian men is diagnostic of the validity of the stereo-type. That is to say, if you interview Italian men and find one who is not a great lover, you will have shown that the stereotype is false. However, choosing Options 3 or 2 is not diagnostic or informative, as neither interview result logically proves or disproves that Italian men are great lovers. Learning that some great lovers (Option 3) are non-Italian men has no bearing on whether or not Italian men are. The existence of a very amorous, say, Spanish, Don Juan neither validates nor invalidates the existence of an equally (or more) amorous Don Giovanni. And learning that non-Italian men (Option 2) are not (or are) good lovers has no bearing on whether or not Italian men are; finding out that French men are or are not great lovers is irrelevant.

Surprisingly, the least frequently picked Option 4 is as diag-nostic and informative as the most frequently chosen Option 1. Why so? Because of the logical rule or law of contraposition, which states that if the proposition "A implies B" is true, its contra-positive proposition "not B implies not A" also is true. In terms of the stereotype, this translates as *If you are not a great lover, then you cannot be an Italian man.* So, interviewing men who are not great lovers is a very good strategy; for if you find one nongreat lover who is Italian, you will have shown that the stereotype is false. Not being able to see this readily is an example of a cognitive blind spot.

WHAT DO COGNITIVE ILLUSIONS TELL US ABOUT US?

The foregoing discussion presents a mere sampling of defects of cold, dispassionate cognition. Additional fallacies and many other biases characterizing our cognitive disabilities are described in rele-vant research articles and in most texts dealing with critical thinking. However, some cognitive scientists, such as Gerd Gigerenzer, L.

Jonathan Cohen, and John Tooby, among others, question the basis of the entire cognitive-illusion approach. One objection is that the findings of investigations on such illusions might reflect not on a lack of rationality on the participants' part but rather on a lack of sophistication. Consider the law of large numbers, broken every time someone commits the gambler's fallacy. This law, which the mathematician Jacob Bernoulli rigorously worked out over a period of several years after he had intuited it, was first published by him in 1713. Despite the long time required to complete his formal proof, Bernoulli believed that the law was so obvious that the stupidest person knows it to be true. As revealed by the gambler's fallacy afflicting even fairly bright college students, the law is not as intuitively obvious as Bernoulli assumed. Why then, argues Cohen, would an unsophisticated human unaware of the existence of such a law not also be prone to the gambler's fallacy? According to Cohen, this is an educational flaw, not rational one. However, as I "see" it (from my Platonic viewpoint), like the logical law of contraposition, the mathematical law of large numbers no doubt applied millennia before Bernoulli discovered it and continues to apply in the present, even if it was or is not known. Moreover, Cohen's argument makes one of the important points of the cognitive illusionist: *cognitive illusions are corrigible by education.*

Another objection is that investigations of cognitive illusions are highly artificial, like the staged acts of a magician or the staged entrapments used by law enforcement officials, both deliberately set up to lead persons to think or act in a given way. In contrast to the rarely implemented field experiment conducted in a mundane "natural" setting, any laboratory experiment—which is the standard procedure in experimental research of human behavior and cognition—is likely to be artificial or contrived. A related concern is that the cognitive-illusion research enterprise frames the problems facing the research subject in ways and contexts that dispose toward his or her fallacious reasoning. Although Piatelli-Palmarini counters such objections successfully in many cases, I believe they do carry some merit. As Gigerenzer notes, the human cognitive system evolved in a natural and social ecology that is noticeably removed from the logician's ivory tower, the standard cognitive research laboratory, or the economist's rational-choice think tank. Gigerenzer has shown that, when framed or formatted in ways that take into account constraints characterizing everyday natural or social ecologies, problem solving tends to be less prone to cognitive fallacies. Moreover, in his recent book, *Gut Feelings: The Intelligence of the Unconscious*, Gigerenzer amply illustrates how in a variety of uncertain situations our intuitions based on innate or acquired heuristics can be quite impressive guides for making choices. Our gut feelings can lead to decisions whose consequences are as fruitful as and at times even more fruitful than decisions based on lengthy or laborious rational-choice cogitations. I frankly admit to being biased toward ecological approaches to the study of human behavior and cognitions because such approaches emphasize contextual, system thinking in addition to reductive, algorithmic thinking.

However, as Piatelli-Palmarini notes, the existence of cognitive illusions does point out to us possible flaws in our ecologically based heuristics, concepts, and cognitions. Likewise, visual illusions point out to us curious flaws in our ecologically based perceptions. It should also be noted that some visual illusions are "natural" or, if you will, "ecological" illusions rather than artificial "parlor tricks." For example, we often perceive the moon as larger when it is just above the horizon than when it is at its zenith in the night sky, even though its location above the horizon may be farther away from our view by a few hundred or thousand miles (the radius of the earth) than it is at its zenith. This and other naturally occurring illusions, as well as clever illusions devised in the laboratory, *say something important about how the visual system evolved to work in perceiving its natural or its nonlaboratory environment.* As such, visual illusions have become enormously important tools in laboratory research on visual perception. Similarly, it would pay off not only to look for cognitive illusions that might occur even in an ecologically valid framework (something that Kahneman and Tversky's work, in response to Gigerenzer's objections, began to address), but also to study how "artificial" *cognitive illusions,* such as those cleverly constructed by the cognitive illusionists, *say something important about how the human conceptual system evolved to work in cognizing its natural, nonlaboratory environment.*

For these reasons, I agree with those cognitive scientists who point out that cognitive illusions are symptomatic of our naturally endowed and our culturally acquired concept-forming apparatus. And I agree also with the ecological psychologists that context can affect the extent of the illusions. Either way, the pervasiveness of cognitive illusions paints a fairly pessimistic picture of human reasoning abilities, particularly in the current times when complex and tricky problems, many of which are self-made rather than "natural," face us. A good example, as we saw in the recent worldwide crash of the financial institutions, is the belief firmly held by some economists that the free market is inherently self-correcting and therefore needs no external regulation. Fortunately, a majority of the fallacies and biases underlying these illusions can be corrected by changing the context or by pointing out the obvious (or not-so-obvious) flaws and biases in the reasoning process.

Perceptual illusions, like the moon illusion or the Müller-Lyer or Ebbinghaus illusions shown in Figure 8.11, are also affected by contextual manipulations. For example, if the angles between the shafts and the "arrowheads" and "arrow-tails" in the Müller-Lyer illusion are systematically broadened, the illusion decreases, and when both the arrowheads and arrow-tails comprise lines at right angles to the shafts, the illusion disappears. However, unlike cognitive illusions, visual illusions are not corrigible by acquiring knowledge. Unaltered, they will still have their illusory effect on you. You can satisfy yourself cognitively by proving through countless physical measurements that the lengths of the shafts in the Müller-Lyer illusion or the diameters of the inner disks in the Ebbinghaus illusion are equal. Afterwards you will still experience the illusion and perhaps still delight in experiencing it. But the first time you "see through" a cognitive illusion, you no longer need to suffer its effects. Both a change of context and a change of mind provide reasons for optimism that, in our cold cognitions, we can correct and even eliminate cognitive illusions and the concomitant cognitive blind spots that can often mar our way in the world.

TEN

Cognition Cultural
and Personal
Blinders and Wonders

*The human understanding is no dry light, but receives an infusion
from the will and affections; whence proceed sciences which may be
called 'sciences as one would.' For what a man had rather were true he
more readily believes.*

FRANCIS BACON, *NOVUM ORGANUM*

. . . a worldview *[is] a collection of beliefs, attitudes, and
assumptions that involves the whole person, not only the intellect, has
some kind of coherence and universality, and imposes itself with a
power far greater than the power of facts and fact-related theory.*

PAUL FEYERABEND, *CONQUEST OF ABUNDANCE*

*. . .intellectual objectivity has no deep effect on psychic life. It is
emotionally empty by definition, and thus . . .[i]t can do no more
than mark, with a certain crude efficiency, the givenness of what it
claims to understand.*

DONALD KUSPIT, *THE END OF ART*

Transmitted over millennia from one generation to the next,
culture is a dynamic balance between change and

conservation, between new and pre-existing ways of making sense, and of coming to an understanding, of the world in all of its rich and diverse aspects. For that reason, culture is both fraught with occasional instabilities and yet sustained by discernable persisting regularities. While culture influences and constrains the cognitive development of an individual appreciably, other influences and constraints on personal development are universal and thus trans-cultural. For instance, language is universally constrained by syntax. Moreover, every culture finds expression, ranging from very simple to highly complex, in social organization, technology, art, ethics, and religion. It is variations on these universal leitmotifs that give rise to cultural differences and distinctiveness, that is, to a constrained form of cultural relativism. And it is through such distinctiveness that culture uniquely influences how we "view" the world and how our views guide our conduct. Since each culture, by virtue of its uniqueness, affords a limited access to reality, each one of us remains blind to a substantial remaining portion of reality.

The German word *Weltanschauung* (worldview) expresses such a global yet circumscribed way of culturally conditioned understanding. In significant part, worldviews are expressions of what philosopher Stephen Pepper calls *world hypotheses*. These, in turn, are based on root metaphors that express core foundational or metaphysical beliefs. An example of such a metaphor is animism, the personification of the universe and the attendant belief that behind all of the events in the visible universe is the agency of invisible spirits. Francis Cornford's book, *From Religion to Philosophy*, amply illustrates how pre-Socratic Greek philosophies grew from such root metaphors. Thus, one role of culture is to provide the soil and seed for these metaphors; another may be to foster, on the one hand, the stability that sustains them and, on the other, the changes that uproot or transplant them. Inspired as they are by foundational beliefs, differences among worldviews can be sources of powerful cultural conflicts.

We will return to these weighty, globally significant cultural influences at a later point, but let us first consider how cultural influences on the way we view the world can be expressed at the local and literal ways of seeing. Some of these influences are so subtle that their consequences for how we see or don't see are hard to detect; others are more easily detectable.

LEVELS OF CULTURAL INHERITANCE IN VISUAL PERCEPTION

Culture is not to be confused with civilization. Archeological evidence indicates that ancient societies, such as those of the Middle and Late Paleolithic eras, were clearly cultured. And even extant aboriginal societies, for instance, those found in Australia, have a cultural heritage that goes back tens of thousands of years prior to any civilization. In these societies, the physical environment was part and parcel of their culture, since the surrounding terrain often had sacral or ritual significance. Yet it was also a geophysical datum. Thus, the visual environment in its cultural expressions as well as its natural and its architectural topography influenced how the people in these societies perceived their world.

The same holds true for contemporary cultures. Many of us live in a city or town, and the city or townscape is of course defined by many human-made structures, most typically the buildings, billboards, and so forth, that line a street. Hence, in large part the structure of our visual environment is defined by its architecture. So from the time we are born, we have a very abundant exposure to horizontal and vertical orientations relative to other, for example, oblique, orientations. As a result, we develop what is known in vision science as the "oblique effect," reflected in the fact that our visual acuity tends to be a bit better for vertically and horizontally orientated lines than for obliquely oriented ones. In contrast, individuals such as the Cree Indians, who live in tepee dwellings on the flat plains of Canada and therefore move about in a human-made environment that is rich in oblique orientations compared to horizontal and vertical ones, tend not to show the oblique effect. These are very subtle yet measurable cross-cultural differences of visual perception. The casual observer would not even be aware of these differences; and even if aware of them, the reason for them would not be readily apparent. But to a trained vision scientist, they can be explained on the basis of long-term biases, produced as early as cortical area V_1 of the developing visual system in early infancy, that result from differential exposure to contour orientations found most prevalently in correspondingly different visual environments.

Studies of cross-cultural comparisons of perception have shown that differences in susceptibilities to certain visual illusions such as the Müller-Lyer illusion (see Fig. 8.11) also depend, among other things, on the type of visual environment one is reared in. For example, the "carpentered" urban environments of Europe or North America are characterized by many inside and outside corners. Thus, dwellers in these environments have plenty of visual exposure to contours resembling the arrowtail (inside corners) and the arrowhead (outside corners) in the Müller-Lyer display. Other visual cultures, like those of natives who live in round thatched huts on the flat savannahs of Africa, largely lack such contours in their visual environment. While observers from both cultures experience the illusory difference between the apparent lengths of the vertical shafts of the Müller-Lyer display, the difference is noticeably larger in the observers raised in carpentered urban environments. By the same token, the African natives experience larger illusions in visual displays whose lines are associated perceptually with larger extents or lengths in their visual environments but are not so associated in a carpentered visual environment. In other words, the functional significance of the same straight-line contours differs in the two visual environments, and thus gives rise, at least in part, to different magnitudes of visual illusions. (The contribution is partial, because other variables such as educational level, a cultural factor, and intraocular pigmentation, a hereditary factor, also affect the magnitude of the illusion.) Again, the reasons for these differences are not readily apparent to a naïve observer because they require a theoretical understanding of how the (mis) perception of the size of an object relates systematically to the (mis)perception of its distance. Such hidden reasons demonstrate that the processes underlying these differences occur, so to speak, below the conscious radar, in some innate or acquired functional property of the visual system that is not directly accessible to cognition.

Explanations of other cultural differences in visual perception are more readily accessible. Four examples follow. The first illustrates how styles of visual perception and cognition develop differently depending on structural differences between visual environments. It turns out that when viewing a highly articulated visual scene, individuals in Western cultures, for example, Americans, tend to focus in an analytic way on salient foreground objects, whereas individuals in East Asian cultures, for example, the Japanese, tend to attend more to the global context within which objects are located. Why? Japanese urban scenes contain more objects, are characterized by a higher level of ambiguity, and thus are more complex than their American counterparts. They therefore afford and encourage attention to, and perception of, context to a greater degree than American urban scenes do. In Chapters 4 and 6, we discussed the contribution of inattentional blindness to not seeing. Applied specifically to the current findings, the relative inattentional blindness of Western observers could explain why they are less context sighted than East Asian observers.

The remaining three examples illustrate differences of visual perception in terms of acquired cultural differences of visual interpretation. Linguists Edward Sapir and Benjamin Whorf hypothesized that language, clearly an important cultural factor, can mold or shape our perceptions and/or cognitions of the world. According to them, significant differences among languages ought to manifest themselves in detectable differences in perceptual abilities. Such differences, for example, the ability to make color discriminations, have indeed been found. For instance, vast snowscapes comprise a large part of the Eskimos' visual environment during much of the year. Among some Eskimos, there are numerous names for snow corresponding to the many slight differences in its color. An Eskimo child, growing up in such a linguistic and physical environment, would acquire such visual color distinctions that for, say, a native Houstonian, living as she does with little or no experience of snow, are too subtle to notice. Had she been raised in an Arctic Eskimo culture, she too would no doubt be able to make such distinctions. Moreover, since in most persons language functions are lateralized to the left cerebral hemispheres, one would expect that these Sapir-Whorfian effects should manifest more strongly when visual stimuli are presented in the right rather than in the left visual hemifield. This prediction also has been confirmed, and it also points out what many an environmentalist and cultural relativist fail to "see": how external environmental factors *and* internal anatomical or biological factors *cooperate* in the brain and, thus, in cognitive development.

The third example is taken from cross-cultural studies of perception comparing African and Western observers. Viewing a depiction, shown in Figure 10.1 (left), of a social scene with African individuals, Western observers were more likely to describe the image right above the head of one of the women as a window. In contrast, East African viewers were more likely to describe that woman as carrying a 4-gallon tin on her head. By now you are no doubt aware of why this difference of perception occurs. Open-air markets (and perhaps other occasions of open-air socializing) and individuals carrying various types of containers on their heads are more commonly encountered in East African cultures than in Western ones. Hence, relatively speaking, the Western observers were blind to the tin. Note that the scene, considered strictly as a physical object providing visual stimulation, is identical for the Western and the African observer. What differs between them, however, is the beholder's share, that is to say, the dominant cognitive schemata shaped by the two cultures and used by their respective members to interpret the same visual input. Like perceptual styles, cognitive schemata such as these are durable dispositions, that is, biases, acting on how we see the world.

Now let's look at the swastika depicted in Figure 10.1 (right). An individual who never had a prior encounter with such a visual sign may react to it with neutral shrug. He neither values nor disvalues it. However, to a member of the Jain sect, the swastika is seen as a saintly symbol, while to a Jew who survived the Holocaust, it is seen as a symbol of utter evil. These two differences of perceptual interpretation are profound and are associated with the lasting influence of having been exposed to two profoundly different cultures, one a culture of nonviolence and the other a culture of brutality. Recent brain-imaging findings indicate that value-based modulation of neural responses in human visual cortex to stimuli can occur as early as area V_1. The act of visual cognition is therefore subject to value-driven biases at already the earliest stages of cortical processing.

Figure 10.1. Left panel: A depiction of an East African visual scene. Right panel: A swastika. Each depiction is subject to different cultural visuocognitive interpretations. (Reproduced with permission from Deregowski, 1973.) Image © UNESCO.

CONSEQUENCES OF THE LEVELS OF CULTURAL INHERITANCE

While some cognitive illusions that place limits on the ability to think correctly cut across all cultures, the examples described in the previous section illustrate the important point that specific cultural influences can introduce correspondingly specific perceptual and cognitive biases. Cultural inheritances can be short or long lasting, consequential or inconsequential. The subtle differences in the oblique effect found to exist between Cree Indians living on the Canadian plains and Canadians living in urban centers, although they reflect important long-lasting, stabilized effects of neural development, have hardly more than a purely scientific relevance. Other cultural influences, also of little practical relevance, are short lived. Consider the following example. Figure 10.2 reintroduces the picture of a perceptually ambiguous display, one that typically is seen as a rabbit or as a duck. In my undergraduate perception course, I have used images of this type to demonstrate how cultural influences can, even if only briefly, bias how we see the world. In one class, I show a series of photos and drawings of typical rodents (mouse, gerbil, squirrel, hamster, etc.) embedded within a larger series of images of inanimate objects; in another class, the photos and drawings of rodents are replaced by those of aquatic birds (gull, egret, swan, pelican, and so on). Immediately thereafter, on first exposure to the display shown in Figure 10.2, students in the former class tend to see only the rabbit, whereas students in the latter class tend to see a duck. Both groups of students were temporarily blind to the alternative percept.

However now imagine a person growing up in a culture in which, ever since a toddler's age, she encountered vastly more cute and cuddly small mammals (including rabbits) than birds of any kind. To no one's great surprise, when shown the ambiguous display of Figure 10.2, the higher-level interpretive areas of her visual brain would be more ready and likely to process a rabbit and, thus, to remain cognitively blind to the duck. This is an example of biases that are stable but again of little but personal relevance.

In contrast to these uneventful cultural biases, significant and more readily noticeable cultural consequences, ranging from non-violent celebration to violent protest, arise when the same stimulus or the same visual datum such as a swastika can be perceptually or cognitively interpreted in more than one way. The meanings of such symbols often are entangled with a host of cherished (or despised) beliefs, rituals, and customs that are expressions of a

Figure 10.2. A sketch that gives rise to the bistable percept of a duck or a rabbit.

by-and-large permanent worldview. And frankly said, by adopting a cherished worldview specific to a given culture (or subculture), each of us adopts culturally acquired biases that can prop up true or false beliefs and can have neutral, laudable, or deplorable consequences. Indeed, biases injected at progressively higher or more complex levels of perceptual and cognitive processing are more likely to express themselves in consequential ways by either constricting or expanding the domain over which our cognition ranges.

As noted in the introduction to this chapter, culture is as much a process as a product, a dynamic balance between movement and stability that has the potential of generating conflict. We hear much talk today of the "culture wars"—of the rife conflicts among and between people about such matters as race, class, and gender that have colored public debate for decades. But though the phrase "culture wars," like a lingering miasma, is in the air, and seems unique only to our times, it is nothing new really, if you have a sense of one of culture's many appurtenances, history. As pointed out by physicist Charles Percy Snow in his book *Two Cultures*, even the quiet groves of academe provided no refuge from cultural conflicts some 50–100 years ago, nor do they do now. In fact, *Kulturkämpfe* of one sort or another, like military campaigns, have been going on for millennia, and, like their military counterparts, cultural weapons, for example, the Internet, have become smarter and more powerful in recent times. As long as the studied hindsight afforded by history is obscured by dubious policies of the here and now and by highly valorized ideologies of the future, be they secular or religious, cultural conflicts will continue their hostile, and at times destructive, onslaught. The victims: truth, beauty, goodness, life . . . . The list could be endless.

OH, BUT FOR OUR UNRULY DRIVES AND EMOTIONS!

One may wonder what it is about cultural influences that they should have such powerful effects, be they constructive or destructive. As to the latter, think of the European sports subculture and the notoriety of rampaging soccer hooligans after a defeat—or for that matter a victory—of their favorite team. While a culture may value and promote the ability to engage in cool, rational thought, irrational drives and emotions, at times extremely powerful since they are part of our basic biological constitution, are, as Freud aptly pointed out, only partly reined in by culture. Hence, understanding and adequately addressing the expressions of cultural influences, particularly the virulent ones, are not merely a matter of studying the social context or the errors to which the intellect is prone. Appropriate channeling—or lack thereof—of our drives and emotions also plays a crucial role.

While the worldview that guides and controls our collective behaviors is shaped in conformance to shared intellectual, social, and cultural constraints, each one of us also enjoys at least a limited autonomy, a freedom from such collective determinants and, moreover, from the determinants of our biological nature. Our beliefs and actions are therefore also, as many an ancient and modern person of wisdom has noted, a matter of the will and of the inclinations of the heart, or to put it in current language, a matter of individual choice and affect. Besides cultural, social, and intellectual controls, each of us has some personal control over thought and conduct. By imprudent or judicious exercise of our free will, we can succumb to the depravity of destructive impulses and emotions on the one hand or constructively transcend the limits imposed by our collective culture and our biology on the other. We can choose to think and live in heretofore unknown or untried ways. Conversions from one religion to another, from a violent political ideology to a nonviolent one, from one way of believing about the world to another often result from the power of the intellect and will freely ratifying the inclinations of the heart.

However, lest one think that conferring the stamp of approval is unidirectional from will and intellect to the heart, it turns out that the heart, in turn, ratifies what we think and will. In his book, *Seeing Red*, the psychologist Nicholas Humphrey notes that blind-sight, sensationless vision, is also affectless vision. Blindsight may still have some control over behavior, but in a largely automatic, zombie-like way. Similarly, an automatized way of thinking and behaving can be entirely affectless. As neuroscientist Antonio Damasio points out in his book *Descartes' Error*, however, a healthy human is not merely a rationally or culturally automatized being but also an emotional one. Emotions are vitally important to the normal conduct of our lives. Damasio discusses a man with frontal lobe damage who could rationally follow the steps of an argument and thus also see and dispassionately ratify the purely logical validity of the conclusion, yet for lack of access to appropriate affect, he could not ratify or give assent to this knowledge in terms of an embodied, vital *belief*. The conclusion simply did not feel or seem a compelling guide for attitude or action. In this case, the cold cognition, lacking warm affect, failed to convert to willed changes of behavior. Just as the practical intellect and the will can be blinded by extremely strong emotions, a lack of emotion, as this case exemplifies, in effect also renders the intellect and will blind. The "heat" generated by our drives, motivations, and emotions energizes and actualizes our view of the world.

FALLACIES AND TRUTHS OF HOT COGNITIONS

If I lose a few thousand of *my* dollars in the stock market or at a casino, well, that's too bad for me; but if that money is *our* lost dollars, well, that will negatively affect us both. Besides exploring the fallacies in assessing the statistical properties of the financial world, psychologists interested in social cognition also have dealt with a number of cognitive fallacies resulting from errors committed in making social, interpersonal, as well as intrapersonal assessments of situations and transactions. These fallacies can have especially weighty consequences, given their personal nature. It is one thing to correctly assess the cold and objective risks of, say, a financial decision; it is another to correctly assess its hot personal, interpersonal, and social stakes.

Of the many types of biases of personal and social cognition, let me describe just a few here; a fuller account can be found by consulting the suggested readings list at the end of this book. According to the social psychologist Ziva Kunda, striving for "directional conclusions"—for desired ends—can evoke biases in several ways. For one, it may bias our access to and construction of beliefs about ourselves, about others, and about public and social events and institutions. That is to say, it biases our declarative knowledge base and predisposes us to see ourselves, our loved ones, and our loved institutions and ideas in as positive light as possible. For example, a student whose directional goal is to ace a test might be predisposed to blame an "unclear" professor or textbook for his ultimately poor test performance rather than to attribute it to his own failure to comprehend the subject matter.

Additionally, the directional goal may bias our application of the rules of inference to a given situation, that is, our procedural knowledge base. Again, not surprisingly, it appears that in many arguments and debates, even in scientific ones, individuals will access inferential or evidentiary rules that support their cherished goals. For example, the committed young-earth creationist might use inferential rules and evidentiary rules that are not applicable to the game of science. I once watched a television program in which a young-earther referred to paintings of St. George vanquishing the dragon, as well as to examples of documentably long traditions of pictorial depictions and oral descriptions of dragon-like creatures, as valid evidence supporting the past coexistence of humans and dinosaurs. He has apparently discounted the abundant evidence that contradicts such coexistence. Perhaps he might also discount the weight of inferential chains of reasoning forming the nexus of evolutionary theory and of the entire enterprise of natural science that conceptually ties the subatomic particle to the cosmos. Such discounting, in my opinion, amounts to a form of intellectual amputation or blinding, which, while relatively harmless at the individual level, would at the collective level undo what has been achieved in science and destroy the possibility of continuing science. This dismal possibility suggests that much more is at stake in such situations than the cold, objective assessment of facts. As evidence one need only hear or read the heated counterattacks to creationism from some members of the established scientific community.

So we are back to the relation of hot emotion and affect to cognizing. Is all cognizing rational? Should cognizing and feeling be always separated? On both counts, no. Regarding the first question, feelings and emotions are informative and thus bear cognitive content. When a person experiences fear, s/he is informed about a potentially threatening situation. As noted in Chapters 4 and 5, even nonconsciously processed information can appropriately activate emotional centers in the brain. For instance, a photograph of an angry face that does not register consciously will still appropriately activate fear-responsive areas in the brain. Thus, even at unconscious levels, the emotions "know" something about the environment and can mobilize an organism's resources accordingly. Regarding the second question, I note again what Antonio Damasio's research indicates, namely, that emotions and, if you will, "the heart" embody and thus ratify what the head, intellect, or reason asserts. When it comes to human concerns and evaluations, to paraphrase a sentence from philosopher Paul Feyerabend's *Farewell to Reason*, things must not only *be* rational, they must also *seem* rational. We can replace the word "rational", without losing the sense of the sentence, with any from a list of words containing "just," "honorable," "beautiful," "right," and so forth.

In some circumstances, moreover, as philosopher Paul Thagard has aptly noted, reasoning is and ought to be emotional. For instance, a scientist who is committed to fostering an objective and dispassionate *description of* the natural world can properly be emotionally excited, if not passionate, about pursuing knowledge in his or her area of research. I suspect that even Stephen Hawking, left rather cold by physics, still found this discovery component of physics emotionally exciting and satisfying in his own work. A social reformer committed to fostering an ethical (and rational) *prescription for* the social world is motivated by outrage over various forms of injustice. Emotions, ranging from fear, anger, or guilt on the one hand to love, awe, and joy on the other, are not only sources of information but also powerful motivators and energizers of activity. The carrot and the stick, each in its own way, are effective. As the optimistic-pessimistic saying goes, "We aspire to the stars, but pain moves us."

A superb athlete or ballerina willingly endures pains and privations to achieve greatness in athletic or artistic performance. A desert monk, sometimes referred to as "God's athlete," willingly practices ascesis as a means of spiritual purification. Some scientists or scholars willingly defer immediate pleasures and in their pursuit of knowledge endure the long-haul pains of frustration or of indifference and opprobrium from their peers. Parents willingly undergo privations and discomforts to ensure their children's growth and welfare. Despite differences of goals and motivations, a common thread runs through these no pain–no gain stories: the passion for, the love of, excellence and the experience of joy it brings. And such love is not a mere feeling, it is a coproduction of emotion, determination, and a discipline that is rigorous and at times even severe.

SPEAKING OF LOVE

Amo ergo sum.

ROCCO DE DONATIS, PROTAGONIST IN IGNAZIO SILONE'S *A
HANDFUL OF BLACKBERRIES*

Try to see it my way

THE BEATLES, *WE CAN WORK IT OUT*

So, having arrived at the end of this essay on not seeing, I have also returned to beginnings. I am a visual scientist with primary interests in visual cognition and neuroscience. And like most scientists, although open to knowledge claims, I am trained to take a critical and skeptical stance toward them, to be "tough-minded," rational, empirical, and objective, and to eschew "soft-headed," subjective, or emotional thinking. From a methodological standpoint, that is well and good. However, long before I ever became a scientist, I was, and continue to be, a human being. And humans, as Francis Bacon said, are more than rational and critical intellects; they also are willing and feeling agents.

About a century ago, the philosopher Max Scheler duly noted the importance of emotions and went the extra step of prioritizing the nature of the human *being* by proposing that "[b]efore man is an *ens cogitans*, or an *ens volens*, he is an *ens amans*." He reminds us that the turn to the self-aware subject surpasses the rational ego (Descartes) and the brute will (Schopenhauer) or the vitalized, power-hungry will (Nietzsche), completing its revolution only to return to its beginnings as an act of love (Augustine, Pascal). In his recent book-length essay entitled *On Seeing*, Frank Gonzalez-Crussi put Scheler's thesis this way:

> At the bottom of all the acts of our will, from the simplest to the most complex; at the bottom of every one of our choices; of everything we perform or accomplish; there we shall find the stirrings of the heart. Affect, the interplay of likes and dislikes, i. e., of love and hate, forms the subsoil of the psyche: it is the nourishing turf out of which grows knowledge. For knowledge arises from interest or preference, which are movements [i.e., motivations] of the heart assimilable to love. And because love incites us to know and to act, it is undeniably the progenitor of cognition and will. Thus, in the order of things of the spirit, love is first.

Like the other emotions, love is necessary for informing, for giving shape to, our *being* human and for its expression in our conduct; but, alas, it is not sufficient. Yet neither is reason nor volition sufficient, no matter how logically we think or how strenuously we huff and puff. It takes all three, although often they make for a clumsy *pas de trois*. But when the choreography comes off gracefully, they can express truth, beauty, and goodness—that other perennial trio that marks the peak of human endeavors and renders existence much more than bearable. For want of a better term to describe the cooperative, triune effort of intellect, will, and emotions, I will use the word *passion* or its derivatives. Consider the passion, that combination of intellect, will, and desire, that inspired mathematician Andrew Wiles to single-mindedly and doggedly pursue, over many years and despite occasional setbacks, a proof of Fermat's last theorem. Consider similarly Michelangelo's multiyear labors, the agonies and the ecstasies that gave expression to—and were expressed on (see Figure 8.4)—the ceiling of the Sistine Chapel. Consider the impact that the *com*passion exercised by Mahatma Gandhi or Martin Luther King had on human conduct and on what it means to be human. Their understanding of inequities elicited a righteous sense of indignation and anger to motivate action on behalf of ameliorative changes of human conduct and belief. All but the most cynical or jaded misanthrope would nod, in each of these three examples, to the achievement not only of truth but also of beauty and goodness, not only of beauty but also of truth and goodness, and not only of goodness but also of truth and beauty.

Concurring with Max Scheler and Frank Gonzalez-Crussi, my personal view is that of love, will, and reason, love holds pride of place in being the *primus inter pares*. Yet, as the saying goes, love can be blind. When attaining heights of passion, love and desire (and hate and aversion) are powers that are so strong that they neutralize the counsel of reason and sane judgment. Rare is the person who falls passionately in love without being at least partially blind to the other's flaws. For that reason, it is hard to rationally convince an in-love person to fall out of love. We have here, in Francis Bacon's words, a severe case of "sciences as one would." Similarly, when in uncontrollable circumstances such as a divorce, death, or forced departure, we must detach from a person or a place we love, we become aggrieved, and logical thought is a cold comfort in a world filled with searing stings of grief. And, as many a cognitive psychotherapist knows, in pathological cases of obsessive attachment or of clinical depression, the restoration of clear-headed, rational thinking is very often an arduous and sometimes an impossible task. Here, where anxiety grips tightly and time does not heal and reasons offered fail to help, only a stronger emotion may be a source of deliverance.

Like the other emotions, love is irrational. But, despite Pascal's claim that the heart has its reasons of which reason is ignorant, few would say it is antirational or unintelligible. Else why, in bygone and recent years, would a host of psycho-, anthropo-, neuroendocrino-, and neurophysio-*logical* investigators apply the rational methods of science—with measurable success—to study love's "logic" (and that of emotions)? Reason working according to its logic in one person can recognize the working of reason in another person, even without grasping the how of the underlying mental or brain processes that an army of cognitive scientists currently is studying. My mathematics instructors proved this to be so when they graded my assigned problems favorably (fortunately for me, most of the time). Likewise, although the "logic" of love differs from the logic of reason, love, by recognizing its own logic in others can open the mind's eye compassionately where a fearful and hurtful aversion, at times to the point of hate, has shut it antipathetically. I am saying nothing that has not been said in many other ways before. But it bears repeating, especially during times fraught with cultural conflicts, because while we need to be reminded that love can blind us, we also need to be reminded that it can move us, despite our imperfections, toward new visions or restore us to old ones that are well worth preserving. The following oft-quoted lines from the poem "Love" by the 17th century metaphysical poet George Herbert allude to this truth of love's beckoning to such visions, even and especially in the face of our shortcomings:

> "I, the unkind, ungrateful? Ah, my dear,
> I cannot look on thee."
> Love took my hand, and smiling, did reply,
> "Who made the eyes but I?"

So, returning to my encounter with the Rice University student—let's call her Susan—whom I introduced in the preface of this book, my concluding statement to her now, after almost 25 years of studied hindsight, would be as follows: "No, Susan, to see in the fullest sense of the word, it is not enough to open your eyes; you also must come with an open mind, and don't forget to come with an open heart."

SUGGESTED READINGS

CHAPTER 1

Bartley, W. W., III (1987). Philosophy of biology versus philosophy of physics. In G. Radnitzky & W. W. Bartley, III (Eds.) *Evolutionary epistemology, rationality, and the sociology of knowledge* (pp. 7–45). La Salle, IL: Open Court.

Campbell, D. T. (1960). Blind variation and selective retention in creative thought as in other knowledge processes. *Psychological Review, 67*, 380–400.

Parker, A. (2004). *In the blink of an eye: How vision sparked the big bang of evolution.* New York: Basic Books.

CHAPTER 2

Coren, S., Ward, L. M., & Enns, J. T. (1999). *Sensation and perception.* Chapter 3: The visual system (pp. 50–83). Fort Worth, TX: Harcourt Brace.

Gibson, J. J. (1979). *The ecological approach to visual perception.* Chapter 12: Looking with the head and eyes (pp. 203–222). New York: Houghton Mifflin.

Goldstein, E. B. (2007). *Sensation & perception.* Chapter 2: Introduction to the physiology of perception (pp. 21–43). Belmont, CA: Thomson Wadsworth.

Mather, G. (2009). *Foundations of sensation and perception.* Chapter 6: The physics of vision, light and the eye (pp.159–195). Hove, UK: Psychology Press.

Wolfe, J., Kluender, K. R., Levi, D., Bartoshuk, L. M., Herz, R. S., Klatzky, R. L., & Lederman, S. J. (2006). *Sensation and perception.* Chapter 2: The first steps in vision (pp. 27–45). Sutherland, MA: Sinauer Associates.

CHAPTER 3

Amedi, A., Merabet, L. B., Bermpohl, F., & Pascual-Leone, A. (2005). The occipital cortex of the blind. *Current Directions in Psychological Science, 14,* 306–311.

Gregory, R. L., & Wallace, J. G. (1963). Recovery from early blindness: A case study. In R. L. Gregory (Ed.), *Concepts and mechanisms in perception* (pp.65–129). London: Duckworth.

Bachmann, T., Breitmeyer, B., & Öğmen, H. (2007). *Experimental phenomena of consciousness: A brief dictionary.* New York: Oxford University Press.

Guillery, R. W. (1974). Visual pathways in albinos. *Scientific American, 230,* 44–54.

Hopkins, B., & Johnson, S. P (2003). *Neurobiology of infant vision.* Westport, CT: Praeger Publishers.

Levi, D. M., & Carkeet, A. (1993). Amblyopia: A consequence of abnormal visual development. In K. Simons (Ed.), *Early visual development: Normal and abnormal* (pp. 391–408). New York: Oxford University Press.

Silverstone, B., Lang, M. A., Rosenthal, B., & Faye, E. E. (2000). *The lighthouse handbook on vision impairment and vision rehabilitation.* New York: Oxford University Press.

Vital-Durand, F., Atkinson, J., & Braddick, O. J. (1996). *Infant vision.* New York: Oxford University Press.

von dem Hagen, E. A. H., Houston, G. C., Hoffmann, M. B., Jeffery, G., & Morland, A. B. (2005). Retinal abnormalities in human albinism translate into reduction of grey matter in occipital cortex. *European Journal of Neuroscience, 22,* 2475–2480.

von Senden, M. (1960). *Space and sight: The perception of space and shape in the congenitally blind before & after operation.* London: Methuen.

CHAPTER 4

Bachmann, T., Breitmeyer, B., & Öğmen, H. (2007). *The experimental phenomena of consciousness: A brief dictionary.* New York: Oxford University Press.

Blakemore, C. (1970). Binocular depth perception and the optic chiasm. *Vision Research, 10,* 43–47.

Ganz, L., & Haffner, M. E. (1974). Permanent perceptual and neuro-physiological effects of visual deprivation in the cat. *Experimental Brain Research, 20,* 67–87.

Mitchell, D. E., & Blakemore, C. (1970). Binocular depth discrimination and the corpus callosum. *Vision Research, 10,* 49–54.

Sacks, O., & Wasserman, R. (1987). The painter who became color blind. *New York Review of Books, 34,* 25–33.

Stoerig, P. (1996). Varieties of vision: From blind responses to conscious recognition. *Trends in Neurosciences, 19,* 401–406.

Stoerig, P., & Cowey, A. (1997). Blindsight in man and monkey. *Brain, 120,* 535–559.

Weiskrantz, L. (1997). *Consciousness lost and found: A neuropsychological exploration.* Oxford, UK: Oxford University Press.

Zeki, S. (1999). *Inner vision: An exploration of art and the brain.* Oxford, UK: Oxford University Press.

Zihl, J., von Cramon, D., & Mai, N. (1983) Selective disturbance of movement vision after bilateral brain damage. *Brain, 106,* 313–340.

CHAPTER 5

Useful websites for demonstrations of the short-duration blinding effects used in vision laboratories:

attentional blink:

http://www.cs.kent.ac.uk/people/rpg/pc52/AB_Webscript/blink.html

binocular-rivalry suppression:

http://psych-s1.psy.vanderbilt.edu/faculty/blaker/rivalry/BR.html

change blindness:

http://viscog.beckman.illinois.edu/djs_lab/demos.html

http://www.uni-mannheim.de/fakul/psycho/irtel/pxlab/demos/

continuous flash suppression:

http://www.klab.caltech.edu/~naotsu/CFS_color_demo.html/

inattentional blindness:

http://viscog.beckman.illinois.edu/djs_lab/demos.html

metacontrast (backward) masking:

http://www.uni-mannheim.de/fakul/psycho/irtel/pxlab/demos/
(under backward masking)

other masking phenomena:

http://macknik.neuralcorrelate.com/

motion-induced blindness:

http://www.echalk.co.uk/amusements/OpticalIllusions/illusions.htm
http://www.metacafe.com/watch/358665/motion_induced_blindness/
http://www.michaelbach.de/ot/

object-substitution (common-onset) masking:
http://www.sfu.ca/~enzo/os16_600/os16_600.html

Alais, D., & Blake, R. (2005). *Binocular rivalry.* Cambridge, MA: MIT Press.

Bachmann, T., Breitmeyer, B., & Öğmen, H. (2007). *Experimental phenomena of consciousness: A brief dictionary.* New York: Oxford University Press.

Biederman, I. (1987). Recognition-by-components: A theory of human image understanding. *Psychological Review, 94,* 115–147.

Bonneh, Y. S., Cooperman, A., & Sagi, D. (2001). Motion-induced blindness in normal observers. *Nature, 411,* 798–801.

Breitmeyer, B. G., & Öğmen, H. (2006). *Visual masking: Time slices through conscious and unconscious vision.* Oxford, UK: Oxford University Press.

Di Lollo, V., Enns, J. T., & Rensink, R. A. (2000). Competition for consciousness among visual events: The psychophysics of reentrant visual processes. *Journal of Experimental Psychology: General, 129,* 481–507.

Enns, J. T., & Di Lollo, V. (2000). What's new in visual masking? *Trends in Cognitive Sciences, 4,* 345–352.

Kim, C.-Y., & Blake, R. (2005). Psychophysical magic: Rendering the visible 'invisible'. *Trends in Cognitive Neuroscience, 9,* 381–388.

Kuhn, G., Amlani, A. A., & Rensink, R. A. (2008). Towards a science of magic. *Trends in Cognitive Sciences, 12,* 349–354.

Levi, D. M. (2008). Crowding—an essential bottleneck for object recognition: A mini-review. *Vision Research, 48,* 645–654.

Macdonald, J. S. P., & Lavie, N. (2008). Load induced blindness. *Journal of Experimental Psychology: Human Perception and Performance, 34,* 1078–1091.

Mack, A., & Rock, I. (1998). *Inattentional blindness.* Cambridge, MA: MIT Press.

Macknik, S. L., King, M., Randi, J., Robbins, A., Teller, Thompson, J., & Martinez-Conde, S. (2008). Attention and awareness in stage magic: Turning tricks into research. *Nature Reviews Neuroscience, 9,* 871–879.

Martinez-Conde, S., & Macknik, S. L. (2008). Magic and the brain. *Scientific American, 299,* 72–79.

Rensink, R. A., O'Regan, J. K., & Clark, J. J. (2000). On the failure to detect changes in scenes across brief interruptions. *Visual Cognition 7,* 127–145.

Shapiro, K. (2001). *The limits of attention: Temporal constraints in human information processing.* Oxford, UK: Oxford University Press.

Simons, D. J., & Chabris, C. F. (1999). Gorillas in our midst: Sustained inattentional blindness for dynamic events. *Perception 28,* 1059–1074.

Simons, D. J., & Rensink, R. A. (2005). Change blindness: Past, present, and future., 9, 16–20.

Wilke, M., Logothetis, N. K., & Leopold, D. A. (2003). Generalized flash suppression of salient visual targets. *Neuron, 39,* 1043–1052.

CHAPTER 6

Behrman, M., & Avidan, G. (2005). Congenital prosopagnosia: Face-blind from birth. *Trends in Cognitive Sciences, 9,* 180–187.

Behrman, M., Peterson, M. A., Moscovitch, M., & Suzuki, S. (2006). Independent representation of parts and relations between them: Evidence from integrative agnosia. *Journal of Experimental Psychology: Human Perception and Performance, 32,* 1169–1184.

Calder, A. J., & Young, A. W. (2005) Understanding the recognition of facial identity and facial expression. *Nature Reviews Neuroscience, 6,* 641–651.

Coltheart, M. (1980). Iconic memory and visible persistence. *Perception & Psychophysics, 27,* 183–228.

Desimone, R., & Ungerleider, L. G. (1989). Neural mechanisms of visual processing in monkeys. In F. Boller & J. Grafman (Eds.) *Handbook of neuropsychology* (Vol. 2, pp. 267–299). New York: Elsevier.

Duchaine, B. C., & Nakayama, K. (2006). Developmental prosopagnosia: A window to content specific face processing. *Current Opinion in Neurobiology, 16,* 166–173.

Ellis, A. W., & Young, A. W. (1988). *Human cognitive neuropsychology.* Hove, UK: Lawrence Erlbaum.

Farah, M. J. (2004). *Visual agnosia* (2nd Ed.). Cambridge, MA: MIT Press.

Fahle, M., & Greenlee, M. (2003). *The neuropsychology of vision.* Oxford, UK: Oxford University Press.

Harrison, S. A., & Tong, F. (2009). Decoding reveals the contents of visual working memory in early visual areas. *Nature, 458,* 632–635.

Humphreys, G. W. (1999). *Case studies in the neuropsychology of vision.* Hove, UK: Psychology Press.

McNeil, J. E., & Warrington, E. K. (1973). Prosopagnosia: A face-specific disorder. *Quarterly Journal of Experimental Psychology, 46,* 1–10.

Pitcher, D., Charles, L., Devlin, J. T., Walsh, V., & Duchaine, B. (2009). Triple dissociation of faces, bodies, and objects in *extrastriate* cortex. *Current Biology, 19,* 319–324.

Sacks, O. (1998). *The man who mistook his wife for a hat: And other clinical tales.* New York: Touchstone.

Serences. J. T., Ester, E. F., Vogel, E. K., & Awh, E. (2009). Stimulus-specific delay activity in human primary visual cortex. *Psychological Science, 20,* 1–8.

Sligte, I. G., Scholte, H. S., & Lamme, V. A. F. (2009). V4 activity predicts the strength of visual short-term memory representations. *Journal of Neuroscience, 29,* 7432–7438.

Sperling, G. (1960). The information available in brief visual presentations. *Psychological Monographs, 74,* Whole No. 498, 1–29.

Sperling, G. (1963). A model for visual memory tasks. *Human Factors, 5,* 19–31.

Sperling, G., Budiansky, J., Spivak, J. G., & Johnson, M. C. (1971). Extremely rapid visual search: The maximum rate of scanning letters for the presence of a numeral. *Science, 174,* 307–311.

Ungerleider, L. G., Courtney, S. M., & Haxby, J. V. (1998). A neural system for human visual working memory. *Proceeding of the National Academy of Sciences USA, 95,* 883–890.

CHAPTER 7

Gheri, C., Chopping, S., & Morgan, M. J. (2008). Synaesthetic colours do not camouflage form in visual search. *Proceedings of the Royal Society B, 275,* 841–846.

Haber, R. N., & Haber, R. B. (1964). Eidetic imagery I: Frequency. *Perceptual and Motor Skills, 19,* 131–138.

Hubbard, E. M., Arman, A. C., Ramachandran, V. S., & Boynton, G. M. (2005). Individual differences among grapheme-color synesthetes: Brain-behavior correlations. *Neuron, 45,* 975–985.

Hubbard, E. M., & Ramachandran, V. S. (2005). Neurocognitive mechanisms of synesthesia. *Neuron, 48,* 509–520.

Kim, C.-Y., Blake, R., & Palmeri, T. (2006). Perceptual interactions between real and synesthetic colors. *Cortex, 46,* 195–203.

Kosslyn, S. M., Thompson, W. L., & Ganis, G. (2006). *The case for mental imagery.* Oxford, UK: Oxford University Press.

Leask, J., Haber, R. N., & Haber, R. B. (1969). Eidetic imagery II: Longitudinal and experimental results. *Psychonomic Science Monographs, 3,* No. 3 (Whole No. 35), 25–48.

Niimi, R., & Yokosawa, K. (2009). Three-quarter views are subjectively good because object orientation is uncertain. *Psychonomic Bulletin & Review, 16,* 289–294.

Pylyshyn, Z. W. (2002). Mental imagery: In search of a theory. *Behavioral and Brain Sciences, 25,* 157–238.

Pylyshyn, Z. W. (2006). *Seeing and visualizing: It's not what you think.* Cambridge, MA: MIT Press.

Ramachandran, V. S., & Hubbard, E. M. (2001). The phenomenology of synesthesia. *Journal of Consciousness Studies, 10,* 49–57.

Shephard, R. N., & Cooper, L. A. (1982). *Mental images and their transformations.* Cambridge, MA: MIT Press.

Shephard, R. N., & Metzler, J. (1971). Mental rotation of three-dimensional objects. *Science, 171,* 701–703.

Torey, Z. (1999). *The crucible of consciousness: A personal exploration of the conscious mind.* New York: Oxford University Press.

Zihl, J. (2000). *Rehabilitation of visual deficits after brain injury.* Hove, UK: Psychology Press.

CHAPTER 8

Attneave, F. (1971). Multistability in perception. *Scientific American, 225,* 63–71.

Elkins, J. (1999). *Why are our pictures puzzles?* New York: Routledge.

Gombrich, E. H. (1972). *Art and illusion: A study in the psychology of pictorial representation.* Princeton, NJ: Princeton University Press.

Harmon, L. (1973). Identifying faces. *Scientific American, 229,* 71–82.

Harmon, L., & Julesz, B. (1973). Masking in visual recognition: Effects of two-dimensional noise. *Science, 180,* 1194–1197.

Jones-Smith, K., & Mathur, H. (2006). Fractal analysis: Revisitng Pollock's drip paintings. *Nature, 444,* E9–E10.

Kanizsa, G., & Gerbino, W. (1982). Amodal completion: Seeing or thinking? In J. Beck (Ed.), *Organization and representation in perception* (pp. 167–190). Hillsdale, NJ: Lawrence Erlbaum Associates.

Kubovy, M. (1986). *The psychology of perspective and renaissance art.* New York: Cambridge University Press.

Murray, M. M., Foxe, D. M., Javitt, D. C., & Foxe J. J. (2004). Setting boundaries: Brain dynamics of modal and amodal illusory shape completion in humans. *Journal of Neuroscience, 24,* 6898–6903.

Sekuler, A. B., & Palmer, S. E. (1992). Perception of partly occluded objects: A microgenetic analysis. *Journal of Experimental Psychology: General, 121,* 95–111.

Shepard, R. N. (1990). *Mindsights.* New York: W. H. Freeman.

Singh, M. (2004). Modal and amodal completion generate different shapes. *Psychological Science, 15,* 454–459.

Stromeyer, C. F., & Julesz, B. (1972). Spatial frequency masking in vision: Critical bands and spread of masking. *Journal of the Optical Society of America, 62,* 1221–1232.

Taylor, R. P. (2002). Order in Pollock's chaos. *Scientific American, 287,* 116–121.

Taylor, R. P., Micolich, A. P., & Jonas, D. (1999). Fractal analysis of Pollock's drip paintings. *Nature, 399,* 422.

Taylor, R. P., Micolich, A. P., & Jonas, D. (2002). The construction of Pollock's fractal drip paintings. *Leonardo, 35,* 203–207.

Teuber, M. L. (1974). Sources of ambiguity in the prints of Maurits C. Escher. *Scientific American, 231,* 90–104.

Zeki, S. (1999). *Inner vision: An exploration of art and the brain.* Oxford, UK: Oxford University Press.

CHAPTER 9

Gigerenzer, G. (2007). *Gut feelings: The intelligence of the unconscious.* New York: Viking.

Gigerenzer, G. (2008). Why heuristics work. *Perspectives on Psychological Science, 3,* 20–29.

Kahneman, D., Slovic, P., & Tversky, A. (1982). *Judgment under uncertainty: Heuristics and biases.* New York: Cambridge University Press.

Kahneman, D., & Tversky, A. (1979). Prospect theory: An analysis of decisions under risk. *Econometrica, 47,* 313–327.

Kahneman, D., & Tversky, A. (1996). On the reality of cognitive illusions. *Psychological Review, 103,* 582–591.

Kahneman, D., & Tversky, A. (2000). *Choices, values and frames.* New York: Cambridge University Press.

Piatelli-Palmarini, M. (1994). *Inevitable illusions.* New York: John Wiley & Sons.

Stent, G. S. (1978) *Paradoxes of progress.* San Francisco: W. H. Freeman.

Todd, P. M., & Gigerenzer, G. (2007). Environments that make us smart. *Current Directions in Psychological Science, 16,* 167–171.

CHAPTER 10

Amodia, D. M., Jost, J. T., Master, S. L., & Yee, C. M. (2008). Neurocognitive correlates of liberalism and conservatism. *Nature Neuroscience, 10*, 1246–1247.

Bodenhausen, G. V., Macrae, C. N., & Hugenberg, K. (2003). Social cognition. In I. Weiner (Ed.), *Handbook of Psychology* (Vol. 5, pp. 257–282). Hoboken, NJ: John Wiley & Sons.

Cohen, J. D. (2005). The vulcanization of the human brain: A neural perspective on interactions between cognition and emotion. *Journal of Economic Perspectives, 19*, 3–24.

Damasio, A. R. (1995). Descartes' error: Emotion, reason, and the human brain. New York: Harper Collins.

Deregowski, J. B (1972). Pictorial perception and culture. *Scientific American, 227*, 82–88.

Deregowski, J. B (1973). On seeing a picture for the first time. *Leonardo, 9*, 19–23.

Drivonikou, G. V., Kay, P., Regier, T., Ivry, R. B., Gilbert, A. L., Franklin, A., & Davies, I. R. L. (2007). Further evidence that Whorfian effects are stronger in the right visual field than the left. *Proceedings of National Academy of Sciences, 104*, 1097–1102.

Ferrari, V., Codispotti, M., Cardinale, R., & Bradley, M. M. (2008). Directed and motivated attention during processing of natural scenes. *Journal of Cognitive Neuroscience, 20*, 1753–1761.

Gregory, R. L. (1997). *Eye and brain.* Princeton, NJ: Princeton University Press.

Kunda, Z. (1990). The case for motivated reasoning. *Psychological Bulletin, 108*, 480–498.

Miyamoto, Y., Nisbett, R. E., & Masuda, T. (2006). Culture and physical environment. *Psychological Science, 17*, 113–119.

Nisbett, R. E., & Miyamoto, Y. (2005). The influence of culture: Holistic versus analytic perception. *Trends in Cognitive Sciences, 9*, 467–473.

Segall, M. H., Campbell, D. T., & Herskovits, M. J. (1966). *The influence of culture on visual perception.* Indianapolis, IN: Bobbs-Merrill.

Serences, J. T. (2008). Value-based modulations in human visual cortex. *Neuron, 60*, 1169–1181.

Tan, L. H., Chan, A. H. D., Kay, P., Khong, P.-L., Yip, L. K. C., & Luke, K.-K. (2008). Language affects patterns of brain activation associated with perceptual decision. *Proceedings of National Academy of Sciences, 105*, 4004–4009.

Thagard, P. (2006). *Hot thought: Mechanisms and applications of emotional cognition.* Cambridge, MA: MIT Press.

Whitson, J. A., & Galinsky, A. D. (2008). Lacking control increases illusory pattern perception. *Science, 322,* 115–117.

EPILOGUE

Bartels, A., & Zeki, S. (2000). The neural basis of romantic love. *NeuroReport, 11,* 3829–3834.

Bartels, A., & Zeki, S. (2004). The neural correlates of maternal and romantic love. *NeuroImage, 21,* 1155–1166.

LeDoux, J. (1998). *The emotional brain: The mysterious underpinnings of emotional life.* New York: Simon & Schuster.

Sternberg, R. J., & Weis, K. (2006). *The new psychology of love.* New Haven, CT: Yale University Press.